The Golden Age of Canadian Figure Skating

The Golden Age of
Canadian Figure Skating

David Young

Summerhill Press Ltd.
Toronto

© 1984 David Young

Published by Summerhill Press Ltd.
Toronto, Ontario

Cover Art: Janet Wilson
Cover Design: Brian Moore
Editor: Judith Drynan

ISBN 0-920197-04-3

Canadian Cataloguing in Publication Data

Young, David, 1930-
    The Golden Age of Canadian Figureskating

Includes index.
ISBN 0-920197-04-3

1. Skaters - Canada - Biography - I. Title.

GV850.A2Y68 1984   796.91'092'2   C84-099434-6

Distributed in Canada by:
Collier Macmillan Canada Inc.
50 Gervais Drive
Don Mills, Ontario M3C 3K4

Printed and bound in Canada by John Deyell Company

To Rowena and Megan

Preface

Figure skating is one of our most successful sports. Internationally, Canada is recognized as having the largest skating organization in the world with nearly 160,000 skaters registered with the Canadian Figure Skating Association, and have earned a reputation for innovation and the pursuit of excellence. Although far removed from the European skating centers, Canada made major contributions to the early development of the sport, and has, since World War II, played an increasingly important role not only on the ice, but also in judging and administration.

While this book is not intended to be a history of skating in Canada, it does throw light on some of the giants of the sport who brought fame to the country and pleasure to millions. Sadly, like many Canadians, they are lionized more elsewhere than at home. The quality of our coaches is renowned, and I personally have been approached in many countries and asked if I know this or that coach. I hope that the following pages will give them some of the recognition they deserve.

In compiling the book I have received unstinted help from many sources: judges like Jane Garden who took phone calls late into the night and dug through protocols left by her father; coaches like Wallace Distelmeyer, Ellen Burka, Osborne Colson and Ray Lockwood, who could always find time to fill in gaps in research with personal anecdotes culled from years of experience as teachers and competitors; and of course from the skaters themselves.

But my greatest encouragement and aid has come from Sheldon Galbraith, who has the qualities that all great teachers possess — the ability to analyse, interpret and communicate, and to remain overall a very human and enjoyable person. Like so many skaters I am permanently in his debt.

My thanks also go to Cecil Hedstrom, her sister Maude McDougall, son Ted Gooderham, their cousin Osborne Colson, and former skating partner Jack Eastwood, for so many hours of entertaining reminiscing. Others who have helped make this book

possible are Donald Jackson, Norris Bowden, Frances Dafoe
Melenick, Norman Melenick, Dr. Suzanne Francis, Margaret
Kenney, June Alltree, Hilda Stamp, Rick O'Neill, Petra Burka,
Vern Taylor, Gloria Magnussen, David Bell, Barbara Gratton Kel-
ly, Ed Deratney, Sandra Markham who helped with the research
when the going was hot, and the public relations department of the
CFSA who spent many hours searching for protocols.

Lastly my thanks to the staff of the Toronto Cricket Skating
and Curling Club for their unfailing courtesy and consideration.

David Young
Toronto 1984

Table of Contents

Introduction

The Golden Age of Canadian figure skating can realistically be placed between 1947, when Barbara Ann Scott won the World Championship, and 1973. During that period, Canada won forty-four world and Olympic medals, twelve of them gold.

Canadian skaters, from Jackson Haines who invented the sit spin, to Donald Jackson who leapt to new heights with the first-ever competitive triple Lutz, have inspired the skaters of the world and spurred them on to greater feats of skill. The first death spiral with the girl's head touching the ice was performed at the 1948 Winter Olympics by the Canadian pair, Morrow and Distelmeyer, and although the achievement was all but lost in the sensational swirl surrounding Barbara Ann, this method of doing one of the most beautiful moves in skating has now become part of every pair's programme in every country. Toller Cranston captured the world's attention when he burst, black-swathed, onto the ice. His highly individualistic and artistic approach to the sport was controversial but never boring, and many believe it had a decided influence on the programmes of other young skaters. In 1978, Vern Taylor successfully threw off the world's first triple Axel, and more recently, Underhill and Martini have amazed audiences with spectacular spins and throws.

From the days of the "gentleman skater" to the modern era of televised performances and fierce competition for careers, skating has remained a highly emotional endeavor. It is unlike any other sport, combining the beauty of the dance with the athletic flights of the gymnast. It appeals to us on many levels. We admire the strength which goes into the incredible leaps and jumps, we are moved by the emotional interpretation of the music, and we experience, as in a dream, the freedom of flight the skaters convey.

The physical and artistic perfection of the competitors is universally felt — they belong to us all eventually. And that is how it should be in this strange mix of movement and strength . . . a gift to the people from the skaters themselves. This is how it has been with the Canadian skaters who have seen the good times and the bad times and still stayed in the game, giving more than they realized to their fellow artists and to those of us whose lives are more earthbound.

Many people wonder what they are after: these skaters who have spent their early lives in constant practice, giving up a normal life for one of dedication and concentration, continuing, as they grow older, to go to early morning sessions before work or school, then returning again to spend every spare minute in the pursuit of the brass ring, the gold medal. Some would say that they need the attention, the praise, and the eventual career, but wiser ones know this is only a small part of it. The skater's dedication is, rather, a quest for the seemingly unattainable, a desire for perfection, and a love of beauty — three things which have always distinguished the strange species of homo sapiens.

The former champions, on a practical level, maintain that skating has enriched their lives by providing a discipline and an ability to achieve goals. Sometimes, however, they must also remember the sweet sound of a blade swooshing through ice in the quiet of a deserted rink. They must experience in their minds the heart-thumping moments just before a free skating event, when years of training would be distilled into single seconds of meaning in front of millions of people — beauty as haiku on the ice. They must recall the elation of a perfectly landed jump, the responsibility of representing the people back home, the ultimate joy of winning.

The Golden Age was from 1948 to 1973, but for many of us, as long as there are skaters pushing forward into new territories and providing us with dreams of grace, the golden years will go on forever.

Judith Drynan
Editor

1

Spring in February

In February, 1947, a young athletic beauty from Ottawa won a gold medal in the World Figure Skating Championships and ushered in the Golden Age of Canadian Skating. Since the competition had begun in 1896, this prize had eluded North Americans, but now, in Stockholm, Sweden, a petite dynamo of the ice named Barbara Ann Scott had skated her way to victory and raised the hopes and spirits of her fellow Canadians.

It was a Saturday — a grey day in a grey world. A world just starting to recover from the ravages of the most devastating conflict in the history of mankind, yet long over the euphoria of the postwar celebrations. A world facing changes in the very fabric of life, as the established order rocked precariously, and new rules and boundaries were drawn up. People were waiting for the first sign of spring, for a symbol of better times to come, for a touch of romance.

In Toronto, that February Saturday was cold. Swirling snow-flurries had followed early morning freezing rain, and shoppers who ventured out to Loblaws or Dominion for choice beef liver at 27¢ a pound, prime rib roast and sirloin steak at 39¢ and 49¢ a pound, struggled from store to streetcar, heads bent against the wind. Even automobiles, for those lucky enough to own them, had no heaters, or ones that either caused fires or took fifteen minutes to warm up. Walkers were plagued by furry tongues caused by the residue in the air from thousands of banked coal fires. Nothing, it seemed, could take the bite out of winter.

For those who could afford it, of course, there were curling clubs and skating, but in an era before developed ski resorts, indoor sports facilities, health clubs and television, winters seemed longer and harder. Most people had to endure or fight the season rather than utilize its special features, so the popularity of entertainments like ice shows and carnivals was at its peak. A week earlier, the Ice Follies of 1947 had played to packed houses at Maple Leaf Gardens, and was actually sold out four days before opening night.

Well, if you couldn't get into the ice show, you could always keep warm at the movies. Bogie, in "The Treasure of Sierra Madre", was at the Tivoli on Eglinton, and Ginger Rogers and Cornel Wilde were at Shea's. The Royal Alex had the film, "Mourning Becomes Electra" — written by Eugene O'Neill and starring local actor Raymond Massey — with seats ranging from 60¢ (front rows at the matinee) to $1.80 (best in the house, evening showing). Live entertainment was provided by Spike Jones and his Musical Depreciation Revue at the Coliseum and, at the Mutual Arena, there was dancing to Ellis McLintock and his Orchestra.

Still, it was a grey day that Saturday when the Toronto Daily Star carried a twenty-eight line story from Stockholm headed: BARBARA SCOTT ONLY FOUR MINUTES FROM ICE TITLE.

Grey, but positively balmy compared to the weather in Sweden where the temperatures hovered at -20° Fahrenheit. That year, the World Championships were held outdoors on an open rink in the middle of a soccer field. It was so cold that the judges sat with their feet in large baskets containing hot rocks, sauna style. There was no protection for the skaters, though, as they jumped and twirled in the frigid air. Barbara Ann competed in an outfit of French blue lamé trimmed with rhinestones, which appeared far more suitable for the débutante's life she had left behind than the rigors of a Scandinavian winter. However, one writer was moved to gush that the dress was "like a frosty night sky with a shiver of stars." Unfortunately, the stars weren't the only ones shivering.

Under those conditions, Barbara Ann's triumph was doubly impressive, but no surprise to enthusiastic followers of figure skating — merely the confirmation of a promise which had been underlined again and again since she had first started competing. At eleven, she had become Junior Champion of Canada, and by the time she was fifteen, the National Champion. Three years later, as the North American champion and three-time Canadian champion, Barbara Ann had already put in more than 20,000 hours practicing school figures and free skating, and just a few weeks before her World bid, she had won the coveted European Championships in Davos, Switzerland.

Along the way, she collected many awards, titles and records — and a special gift from one of her idols. It was when Barbara Ann was ten, and already holding her gold figure skating test medal, that she met the woman she hoped to emulate and succeed on the ice — the great Sonja Henie, ten times World champion and three times Olympic champion.

Miss Henie took Barbara Ann out to tea and gave her an autographed picture of herself, in the tradition started for her by Papa Henie when the eleven-year-old Sonja first competed at the Olympics in 1924. This time, however, she celebrated the importance of the occasion by enclosing the picture in a gold frame. She could afford it. Not only was she the highest paid professional skater the world had ever known, she had also garnered earnings that would have sent some of today's pros running to their agents with their toes curled. These earnings were thinly described as expenses for herself, of course, and papa and mama, but also for her brother, her trainer, her maid, her dog, and her parrot.

Barbara Ann had never shared this quest for a glamorous lifestyle — she had always professed herself a homebody — but she did share the ambition of the younger Sonja Henie to become an Olympic champion. She was to achieve that goal, inspiring generations of skaters to go on to victory and make figure skating Canada's most successful international sport. Millions of people throughout the world, many of whom would never actually see her skate, would revere her talent, beauty, and determination. Growing showmanship on the ice was to have a dramatic effect on styles, judging, and, eventually, the marking systems in competitions.

But first came the prize at the World Championships, and with that golden win, Canada had a new heroine. The touch of spring had arrived — a new era in skating had begun. A time when the question would not be "Will we win a medal?" but "How many will we get?", when the Canadian team was one to be feared and rival coaches and trainers would try every trick in the book to defeat our champions, when Canadian officials learned some of the hard facts of life about the bargaining and exchanging of favors, and a time when champions from around the world made Canada their mecca for summer training.

The country had a heroine, but seemed reluctant to recognize the heroes who had come before, and this reluctance submerged the stories of some of the predecessors of Barbara Ann who set the pace in the early days of skating competition, and those in more recent times who helped prepare the way in international circles for Canada to gain recognition as a skating nation to be reckoned with.

DOLLS SHOP

CARNIVAL
TORONTO SKATING CLUB
ARENA GARDENS
MARCH 24 TH   1922

**Skating Carnivals played an important role in the development
of Canadian skaters.**

2

Origins of Showmanship

Ice skating was centuries old before Barbara Ann got her first pair of blades. In fact, there were references to the activity over fifty years before William the Conqueror carried out the last successful invasion of England in 1066, and Salmund the Wise, of Icelandic fame, mentioned it in 1100. Two hundred years later, Holland adopted a patron saint to oversee the interests of skaters, and by the year 1500 Dutch artisans were using iron skates with turned-up toes.

The first book totally devoted to skating, "A Treatise on Skating" by Robert Jones, appeared in 1772 in England. It sold incredibly well, and nearly one hundred years later had been reprinted ten times. The book described many movements familiar to modern skaters like the inside and outside circle, the outside foreward eight, and the figure of the heart skated on one leg.

Although the Iroquois Indians were using skates made of bone to help them hunt down their quarry in winter, the first clear record of skating in Canada was by Pierre du Gau, of the Sieur de Monts' expedition to Acadia in 1604. After he landed a small force of settlers on the island of St. Croix in the Bay of Fundy, he wrote: "During the winter some of the young men went hunting in spite of the cold weather. They went skating on ponds." One of the young men on the expedition was Samuel de Champlain who, five years later, founded the settlement of Quebec.

In the 18th century, the sport had spread to the civilian population of Upper Canada, thanks largely to British army officers who introduced skating as a recreation as well as a means of transportation. In 1794, the Governor's wife, Mrs. Simcoe, and a group of friends, helped break the monotony of winter and "drove to the Donn to see Mr. Talbot skate." How well he performed we don't know, but by the time Queen Victoria came to the throne in 1837, skating was a recognized Canadian winter pastime, and her name was to grace some of the most famous skating clubs in the country.

Soon technology and new techniques led to improvement in skate design and increased demand, and where there's demand, private enterprise is never far behind. Skating went commercial. Pay-as-you-skate was introduced, and entrepreneurs, anticipating the need for better ice surfaces, wooed the enthusiasts away from the rivers, lakes and ponds.

A rink in Toronto, forty by fifty yards, was built by O. Wardell and P. Arnold with an adjoining skate and boot house for the convenience of the gentry. The less fortunate were kept out by a high fence, to deter peeking and climbing over for a free whirl.

In New Brunswick, which prided itself on having the best skating facilities in the world, the conversion to prepared rinks met with some opposition from the hardier skaters, who calmy faced the unsheltered stretches of the St. John River — often covered with glare ice for many miles. One author noted, as late as 1876:

> "From the mouth of river St. John upwards to Fredericton is about 80 miles and skaters frequently accomplish this distance in the day. I skated 150 miles in two days (half in less than six hours) without any feeling of fatigue or stiffness. In one or two straight reaches of the St. John River a good skater with a breeze in his favour can cover 20 miles an hour. The skates used for long journeys differ from the ordinary ones in being much longer and straighter in the iron. The "Acme" and other patent skates, though convenient for rinks are useless for long journeys."

Ten years later, distance enthusiasts using the Long Reach Skates had no problem in completing the eighty-four miles from Fredericton to Indiatown, and six hours was considered a reasonable time, but it was the "useless" Acme skate that changed the style of skating. Before the Acme, the skate had developed from the Iroquois' sharpened bone blades, to a cheap all metal screw and buckle device that could be fitted onto any boot. Its major disadvantage was that the skater had to bore holes into the heels of his shoes with a gimlet to screw on the skate heel. The skate also needed heavy straps and buckles which eventually cramped feet and cut into ankles.

Then John Forbes of Dartmouth, Nova Scotia, solved the problem when he patented the first spring skate. This had clasps activated by a small lever, which gripped the sole and heel of the boot so that the skate could be attached or removed in seconds. In 1861, Forbes opened a small factory in Halifax to manufacture the Forbes Acme Skate. Three years later the company operated in Dartmouth as The Starr Manufacturing Company with a reputation which had grown and moved across the country, into the United States, and across the Atlantic to Europe. Over the years, the skate improved aesthetically with the addition of electroplating, and wealthy patrons often received expensive and elaborate storing cases containing skates plated in nickel or gold. The Governor General, Lord Dufferin, and Lady Dufferin were among titled recipients of presentation sets.

Although the skate's simplicity increased the popularity of the sport, it also encouraged one of the early examples of negative public relations. Manufacturers of ball bearing roller skates played up the element of risk in ice skating, and circulated a message that could well have been prepared for the snowmobilers taking to the frozen lakes a hundred years later.

> "Terrible dangers attend upon this amusement. A skater should ever venture upon water that is beyond his depth, unless he is a good swimmer. Even the ability to swim is not sufficient, for a few minutes immersion in ice-cold water will chill the limbs and paralyze the strength of the strongest swimmer; and unless a ladder, a rope or some means of escape be close at hand he will inevitably sink and rise no more."

The fears of the non-swimmers were assuaged, however, by

the growth of commercial rinks and, in answer to the Canadian climate, the covered rinks and development of the skating clubs. The first covered rink was opened in Quebec City, followed closely in 1859 by one built on the location of the Montreal Skating Club. Three years later, the first Victoria Skating Club was incorporated in Montreal, and the popular Victoria Rink built. The next year an elaborate opening ceremony was staged to unveil a Halifax rink — complete with lighting, heating, and a band platform. By 1870 there were a dozen covered rinks in Canada.

Development was somewhat slower in Toronto, which would eventually lead the country in the production of champions. The Toronto Curling and Skating Club was formed in 1874, later changing to the Victoria Skating and Curling Association (1887), and, after some further name-juggling, finally becoming the Toronto Skating Club in 1913.

With the growth of the covered rinks, skating became quite the thing, and society moved from the ballroom onto the ice, along with fancy dress carnivals, masked balls, and other extravaganzas designed to while away the winter hours.

At Lennoxville, Quebec, the organizers boasted that they had all the usual characters plus Sir Walter Raleigh, Herne the Hunter, Sailor of the Nile, Don Quixote, and a Squaw with Papoose. A Confederation year carnival at Toronto's Victoria Skating Rink included not only the characters, but a "Grand Torchlight Parade" with the band of the Queen's Own Rifles in attendance, and all for twenty-five cents.

In March 1867, hundreds of costumed skaters attended a fancy dress entertainment at Montreal's Victoria Skating Rink, where the decorations vied with the outfits for sheer extravagance. In addition to the normal lighting, there were "eight huge and handsome stained-glass lanterns of Chinese style, two of which were located at either end, with two more at each of the separate galleries occupied by the bands. Suspended from the centre of the roof, there was a large ornamental basket containing flowers and evergreens; and from it colourful festoons extended to the four corners of the building." At the same event, the Club issued this ambiguous rule. "No ontrusion will be permitted on the seats of the Ladies Committee or on those of the lady skaters."

The carnivals were famed for the originality of their costumes, and the social movers of the time spent weeks preparing for a few hours of public exposure. In a masquerade at Sherbrooke, Quebec, the characters included Titania, Mary Queen of Scots, Peasant of the Pyrenees, Dutch Fish Woman, Spanish Lady, Indian Chief, Cinderella's Godmother, Somnambulist, Court Jester, French Cavalier, Zouvae, Patent Drugs, Persian Prince and his Satanic Majesty.

The invention of the artificial ice rink further accelerated the development of the sport. In Chelsea England, in 1876, a mixture of glycerine and water was chilled by ether and circulated by copper pipes, then covered by water, producing an ice surface measuring one hundred square feet.

North America's first artificial ice rink was installed and operated by Thomas L. Rankin in 1879 in New York's old Madison Square Garden. It had an area of six thousand square feet, and on opening night was attended by "hundreds of skaters and thousands of spectators in an environment of innumerable gas jets, scores of coloured lights, and flashes of varied-coloured calcium glares." Europe and the United States continued to build artificial rinks throughout the remainder of the century, but Canada did not have one until 1912, in Vancouver.

At the same time skating had been divided into a number of categories which included figure skating, more popularly known as fancy skating, trick or stunt skating, and speed skating.

While fancy skating developed into a recreation for the well-to-do part of the population, and remained so for nearly eighty years, speed and stunt skating counted more earthy people in its ranks. The speed skaters tended not to specialize too much, and became the core of the first travelling professional skating showmen giving the lead in showmanship to the burgeoning skating carnivals — precursors of the ice shows we know today.

Among the all-rounders was Hugh McCormick from the skaters' paradise, New Brunswick. He was a farm boy whose skates had been made by a blacksmith (of "The Willows" on the Kennebecasis River), and because of his ungainly-looking skates, he became the comic turn of the races. He had the last laugh, though. Not only did he achieve fame throughout all of North America, but he eventually competed against Norway's Axel Paulsen — the accredited international champion, holder of most of the world's records and the man destined to give his name to one of free skating's most popular jumps — and defeated him.

Fred Robson, known as "flash on skates," first tackled the ice at Toronto's Mutual Arena in homemade skates, but by the time he was nineteen, he held nine world records and shared one. After retirement, he won awards in exhibition and trick skating, and established the Canadian record for barrel-jumping by soaring over eleven of them.

Jack McCulloch (1872-1918) was the first athlete from Manitoba to win world renown. His fame came largely from speedskating, but he was also an accomplished hockey player, oarsman, cyclist, sprinter and gymnast, and gave many figure skating exhibitions.

Perhaps the most versatile skater of all time was Norval Baptie — the man who pioneered the ice show. Born in Bethany, Ontario, in 1879, he was unbeaten in speed skating for 16 years, from 1894 to 1910. He won close to five thousand races before he turned to stunt and figure skating, setting records for broad jumping, barrel jumping, skating backwards, and skating on stilts. He also barnstormed his way across Canada and the Northern United States with an ice show consisting of one man — himself. Before his death in 1966, he described this endeavor.

"The show consisted of seven acts. First, I would help the ticket taker at the gate. Then I would loosen up with an exhibition of speed skating, just to get some of the 20 to 30 below zero (F) weather out of my bones.... A fox chase usually followed with as many as fifty local youngsters skating their heads off in an effort to catch me. I would then jump some barrels, and in some of these towns, they had kids who were pretty handy at this, and they wouldn't be satisfied until you upped the number to exceed their best efforts. This would be followed with an exhibition of figure or fancy skating. The finale usually consisted of a stilt-skating exhibition, and mine usually measured twenty-six inches, although most of those used by today's spectacular acts are only fourteen inches high."

The shows were a huge success and, after World War 1, Baptie expanded them into the kind of ice show we see today, taking

Gladys Lamb as his partner for life as well as on the ice.

In the early 1930s, he directed carnivals featuring the reigning world and Olympic champion, Sonja Henie, and in 1938, at age fifty-nine, he retired from active skating, and moved to Washington, D.C. There, he became a professional coach for the Washington Figure Skating Club, and worked alongside former Canadian figure skating champion and professional show skater, Osborne Colson who stated that, "he was one of the most remarkable men I had ever met." And so he proved. In 1954, he lost his left leg because of diabetic complications, and four years later his right leg had to be amputated as well. In spite of this, the skater and competitor in him wouldn't give up. He moved to Baltimore and became a coach — teaching from a wheelchair until his death at age eighty-seven.

Three years before he died, he was given the well-deserved honor of being one of the first skaters, Sonja Henie was the other, named to the United States Ice Skating Hall of Fame.

It was because of the varied talents of men like Robson, McCulloch and Baptie, that different forms of skating continued to be closely entwined.

Jackson Haines, the father of modern figure skating.

3

A Man For All Sports

By the middle of Queen Victoria's reign, the British were circling the fashionable new skating rinks in a way which reflected the moral precepts of the Victorian era in both style and dress.

The skating posture was as stiff as the whalebone corsets that crimped the waists of the women who took to the ice. The body was kept rigid and the legs straight — an almost unbelievable achievement in the eyes of modern day sports instructors whose rallying cry is "bend the knees" — and moving the arms away from the body was considered bad form. There was an overwhelming preoccupation with executing perfect tracings on the ice, and the competitions to demonstrate this technique grew into today's "figures."

Their colonial cousins in North America, when not skating marathons on the frozen lakes and rivers, adopted a style which was slightly less rigid, and consisted of a series of small figures with a predominance of jerky movements by the unemployed leg.

There were, however, nonconformists in the skating world who were willing to break out from under the umbrella of Victorian recitude, and take advantage of the freedom provided by the technological development of the skate. The curved blade now made it possible to advance the execution of movements forwards, backwards, and upwards, combining artistry with athletic skill.

The leader away from rigidity of movement was an expatriot Canadian who worked in New York as a ballet master, Jackson Haines. A century later, the comparisons between him and the great skating innovator Tollar Cranston were so numerous — in style, interpretation of music, appreciation of the arts, and reception by an audience — that Cranston was to wonder aloud if he were, in fact, the reincarnation of Haines.

He originally made his name by marrying the form of ballet to the movements of skating, and, like Cranston, he either thrilled or shocked his audiences with his long-flowing extensions, graceful spirals, lightning jumps, and wildly imaginative costumes. He used skates of his own design, the first to have the steel blades attached to the shoes, and invented the sit spin which became known as the Jackson Haines.

The supporters of the stiff form were horrified, particularly in England, but the general public acclaimed him in Vienna, Budapest, Berlin, Scandanavia, and St. Petersburg, but most of all in Vienna, where he skated a march, a waltz, a mazurka and a quadrille. Free style skating had begun.

The exhibitions by Haines, and other less adept but nonetheless adventurous performers, encouraged sponsors to promote figure skating competitions in Montreal, Hamilton and Toronto — wherever a suitable rink existed. These were grand affairs. The skaters competed for a gold medal or silver cup valued at fifty dollars wholesale, while a military band, and sometimes two, rendered suitable airs to accompany their efforts.

Soon the local competitions grew into national events, and the first American championships were held in 1863, dominated by Jackson Haines. He retained his title the following year and then went on a tour of his home country, Canada. In Toronto, The Dailey Leader enthused:

> "We beg to announce to the Lovers of Skating that we have made arrangements at very great expense with The Champion Skater, Mr. Jackson Haines of New York, to give exhibitions at the West End Skating Pond. Admission 15 cents.
> Those who have not seen him would read with incredulity a description of the extraordinary acts he attempts and accomplishes with so much grace and ease."

It was during this 1864 tour that Haines was seen by the

parents of a three-year-old boy in Montreal, Louis Rubenstein, destined to be another dynamic influence in the development of skating.

As a teenager, he went to Vienna to study skating at the Jackson Haines school, and when he returned to Canada, he taught what he had learned from Haines himself before his death in 1876. He was instrumental in forming the Canadian Amateur Skating Association in 1878, which involved all forms of the sport, but since he did not want to confine his activities to administration, he decided to become a serious contender in skating competitions.

His first recorded appearance as a competitor was in 1879, when, at eighteen years of age, he battled for the top spot with Messrs. Periera and Barlow. A contemporary report in The Montreal Gazette is larded with descriptive phrases like "the pivot figures," "the double forward locomotive steps," "the inside edge cross-roll backwards," and "the cross-cut figure."

In spite of these efforts, Louis came in third with 300 points, behind Periera with 351, and Barlow, 400. The judges demurred:

> "We would have liked to have referred more to Mr. Rubenstein's skating, he being but a beginner compared to his opponents. The form of his figures on the ice was very perfect in many cases, but the difficulty with which he attained the distinction was a bar to his taking the prize."

There were few bars after that appearance. Within four years he had developed power and grace, was the star of the Victoria Club, and the acknowledged champion of The Dominion of Canada. He retained the title until 1889, and was the American Champion in 1888, '89 and '91.

The first World Championship, without benefit of an international skating organization, was held in St. Petersburg (now Leningrad), Russia in 1890. In spite of warnings from friends and family about the virulent anti-Semitism in that country, where relentless pogroms had led to a mass exodus of Jews, nothing would keep Rubenstein away, and when it became obvious that he was determined to go, fellow citizens in Montreal contributed four hundred dollars to finance the trip.

The event was highlighted by the kind of political drama that has become familiar in international sporting events. When Rubenstein arrived in St. Petersburg a month ahead of the competition and confirmed that he was Jewish, although of Canadian birth, he was given twenty-four hours to leave town.

In desperation, he went to the British Embassy to seek help. He had with him a letter of introduction to the British Ambassador Sir Robert Morier, from the Governor General, Lord Stanley of Preston, and Sir Robert acted swiftly. If his old friend Lord Stanley thought so highly of the young skater, he promised to see what he could do.

The next morning, shortly before the deadline, a policeman came to Rubenstein's hotel. The young Canadian was already preparing to leave and thought the policeman was there to escort him out of the city. Instead, he carried the message that the chief of police had decided, as a personal favor to the Ambassador, to let Rubenstein stay until the competition was completed, but no longer.

The pressure built up for the Jewish hopeful for, even though he had been given permission to stay, he was subject to daily harassment by the local police, and kept under constant surveillance.

Also, Rubenstein had learned his skating on indoor rinks and needed time to adjust to the outdoor conditions of wind, cold and hard ice that were to plague competitors for the next seventy years.

Participants in the first world championship had to compete, as today, in three events. The first involved the execution of nine figures selected by the committee, and described in the published circular.

The second event called for the execution of five figures chosen by the competitors, and described in a sealed envelope which they presented to officials before performing.

The third was the equivalent of today's free skating event "limited to 10 minutes duration." (The free skating part of current international competitions is limited to 4.5 minutes).

The method of scoring was complicated. There were three points for perfect execution, two for good, one for tolerable, and none for bad. There were no fractions of points, and in the instructions to judges, there was no mention of deductions for faults, such as touching the ice with the hand or, in figures, putting the second skate down. The scoring for a figure was to be multiplied by

Maude and Cecil Smith work on a foot spiral they developed for pairs competition in 1922. *(top).*

Olympic oath taking. Chamonix 1924.

Melville Rogers and Cecil Smith at practice in London, England, before the 1924 Winter Olympics *(above)*.

Maude Smith and Jack Eastwood, pairs competitors at the 1928 Olympics *(right)*.

Canadian Olympic team 1924. Charles Gorman, speedskater, Cecil Smith and Melville Rogers follow flag bearer.

Montgomery ''Bud'' Wilson left, with Maude and Cecil Smith and Jack Eastwood, Canadian fours champions, 1925-27 *(above).*

Cecil Smith was favorite of North American competitors at the first Winter Olympics. Seen here with two US hockey players.

Sonja 1928

Pappa Henie distributed signed pictures of daughter Sonja to all and sundry at 1928 Olympics *(above)*.

Barbara Ann Scott and Hans Gerschwiler after 1947 European Championships at Davos, 1947 *(left)*.

Barbara Ann, Davos, 1948.

Barbara Ann, St. Moritz, 1948.

Sheldon Galbraith skated Barbara Ann's programme with her during practice for 1948 Olympics in St. Moritz *(above)*.

Barbara Ann warms her boots on radiator at 1947 World Championships in Stockholm *(left)*.

Wallace Distelmeyer and Suzanne Morrow, competing in 1948 Olympics.

Suzanne Morrow, fourth-ranked in the world from 1950-52, and the only woman skater to have held the Canadian senior titles in all divisions.

The 1948 Olympic parade. Barbara Ann Scott foreground, Marilyn Ruth Tate, Suzanne Morrow, Wallace Distelmeyer and Sheldon Galbraith behind *(below)*.

the numerical degree of difficulty, and each figure had to be executed five times on each foot.

The judges were instructed to take special account of skating into place, the method of changing feet, and the degree of ease and grace with which movements were performed.

Rubenstein was a credit to his former coach and displayed masterly control. He demonstrated his ability to retrace a pattern on the ice three or four times without blurring the original outline, and executed his performance with such grace and elegance that the judges were astounded. Despite their hostility to foreigners in general and Jews in particular, they had no choice but to award him the title. In fact the Russians were so captivated by his style that, ironically, he was invited to stay longer and give some exhibitions.

He continued to be fêted throughout Europe, and whenever he took to the ice for practice he was surrounded by admiring crowds. "It was a little bit uncomfortable, because unless skating a match of some sort, a fellow hates to put himself on exhibition. But then there was one thing gratifying. When people asked who we were, they discovered we were Canadians, and I don't think we lowered the reputation of the Dominion as far as skating was concerned. The attention was flattering, and to tell you the truth, I rather liked it."

Flattery and a hero's welcome were about all Rubenstein got for his efforts. Among those who greeted him on his return was Lord Stanley, writer of the important letter. Three years later, this same Lord Stanley bought a fifty dollar trophy for annual presentation to the amateur hockey champions of Canada. It was passed along to the pros in 1910, and since 1926 the Stanley Cup has been the exclusive property of the National Hockey League — vied for annually by hockey teams all over North America. Rubenstein remained active in skating, winning the American title the next year, and going on to judge competitions throughout Canada and the United States. Like many of the early skaters, he was an all-round sportsman. He was an enthusiastic cyclist and president of the Canadian Wheelmen's Association for eighteen years, and is considered by many people to be the father of bowling in Canada.

The Amateur Skating Association of Canada remained the ruling body for both speed and figure skating until 1914, and during this period Rubenstein was secretary and president. He also became president of the International Skating Union of America, formed in Montreal in 1907. This umbrella organization included the National Skating Association of America, which Rubenstein had helped to found, the Amateur Skating Association of Canada, and the Western Skating Association of Chicago.

He represented the St. Louis ward of Montreal as Alderman until his death in 1931, and was involved in all kinds of amateur sports. There were few major events at which the portly, heavily-moustached eminence of skating was not present, gazing — sometimes benevolently, sometimes fiercely — over his pince-nez. Devoted to the pursuit of excellence, he would go to great lengths to meet his objectives and help others meet theirs.

In 1919, approaching his sixtieth year, he was presiding over some young skaters attempting to pass their first test when he became dissatisfied with the loops the competitors were executing. So he went home and returned with his old spring skates, then snapped them on and proceded to demonstrate to the awed students the perfect loops that made him world champion.

Sadly, his achievements are virtually unknown today. In Montreal there is a small memorial, and the Rubenstein Baths were named after him. As one writer said, "No city in the world has contributed more to sport than Montreal, and no Montrealer has ever given more to sport than Louis Rubenstein."

CITIUS - ALTIUS - FORTIUS

VIII OLYMPIADE -- PARIS

Comité Olympique Fr————s

3o. Rue de Grammont - (Paris-Building) ——S (IIe)

CARTE D'IDE—ITÉ

Le Comité Olympique(1) ————ucais

certifie que Mme ——— *Smith*

est (2) ——————— *aux Jeux de*

la VIIIe Olym—— *rganisés à Paris en 1924.*

Le Secrétaire Gé————   Le Président du C.O.F. Commissaire
du Comité Oly————   Général des Jeux de la VIIIe Olympiade,
França——

——) Nationalité du Comité Olympi———
(2) Concurrent ou officie——

**Competitor's identity card issued to Cecil Smith at the first
Winter Olympics in Chamonix, France in 1924.**

4

Demure Benumbed and Breakfastless

In the period after World War I, figure skating in Toronto was still the preserve of the well-to-do. At the Toronto Skating Club, gentlemen wore white gloves to the Saturday afternoon dance sessions, and members were received at the front door of their new indoor rink by a uniformed butler.

Two young women, Cecil and Maude Eustace Smith, entered this world of skating and social establishment almost by accident. Their skating careers began when Cecil was barely nine and her sister eleven. Like many Canadians, then and now, their introduction to the ice had been on local ponds and outdoor rinks.

They belonged to an adventuresome and outgoing family, so it was no surprise that when the girls found the endless circling of frozen ponds too tame, they decided to form a girls' hockey team. "We beat everyone we played," said Cecil, "including all the girls' private schools like Branksome Hall and Havergal, but Bishop Strachan wouldn't play us because we wore pants. The boys' schools backed away too. The Headmasters of St. Andrew's and Trinity wouldn't allow their teams to play against us."

Cecil, pert and pretty, elected herself goal tender, ignoring the risks and possibilities of injury to the wideset eyes which were later to bedazzle Canada's first Olympic hockey champions. Home rink was in the garden of a neighbor, Mrs. Scott Griffin, who insisted that the team sweep and flood their own ice before each game. She also insisted, wisely as it turned out, that the girls attempt some figures as well.

Soon, the Smiths' enthusiasm for figures led them to practice sessions at the outdoor rink of the Toronto Skating Club where members gathered on selected evenings. While there was no indoor facility, the members could change in a room with hot stoves and skate inside a boarded enclosure normally reserved for a local hockey team. Outside skated the general public, including the Smith sisters, until someone from the club saw them and invited them inside the pale.

Their entry into the T.S.C. was fortuitous. At that time, the twelve hundred members had become shareholders in the Winter Club, which invested $135,000 in an indoor club on Dupont Street with a rink made of artificial ice, obtained initially from the refrigeration plant of the adjoining Silverwood's Dairy. This artificial ice surface was to play an important part in deciding who would represent Canada at the first Winter Olympics in 1924.

The Smith girls became dedicated skaters and practiced six hours every day for the five months that the club was open. They travelled to the rink together on the five a.m. streetcar, then returned to St. Clair and walked to classes at Bishop Strachan. After school they repeated the journey.

Success came early. Within a year of the opening of the new facility, Cecil and Maude (nicknamed Jim) became the club's 1921 junior pairs' champions, and the next year Cecil was junior ladies' champion, beating both her sister and Constance Wilson, who was to become a lifetime rival.

Today, a skater is programmed through a series of selective competitions and any number of international events before appearing in front of world judges, but in the nineteen-twenties, club competitions and carnivals were the most common form of preparation.

Media coverage was extensive. A local paper covered a 1922 performance of the ballet pantomime "The Dolls' Shop," which included Norval Baptie and Gladys Lamb as professional performers, and featured Melville Rogers, Cecil and Maude Smith, and the club junior champion Montgomery Wilson.

"The Toronto Skating Clubs' annual carnival means to the community something beautiful in the sense that the Mendelssohn choir does, or the tulips that will soon come in Queen's Park, or the grass on

Rosedale's lawns, or a sunset beyond the Humber — something that is fundamentally fine and striking. It has the stuff of which children's dreams are made, a touch of fantasy, a glint of laughter, a splash of youth, an undercurrent of vitality, joy, grace, light and colour...
Last night's carnival in the Arena was more than a pageant, more than a glorious carnival....it stood as a symbol of all the light, bright, splendid things that lie beneath the harsh exterior of Canada's long winter.''

Then, a brief review of the skating performances.

"And lastly of all, the juniors, the Toronto Skating Club Champions Miss Cecil Smith and Miss Maude Smith (pair) and Master Montgomery Wilson. The two girls in kilts with hair and tartans flying, are beautiful skaters. Young Wilson is a miniature wizard on the ice, not inferior in degree to even the professionals. With the club fostering such talent as these youngsters, it looks as if Toronto will shortly produce some of the very best skaters on the continent.''

Fulsome the writer may have been, but he had the gift of prophesy. The younger Smith sister, Cecil, had proven to be the more talented singles' skater, and by 1923 she was runner-up in the Canadian championships, second only to Dorothy Jenkins who retained the title she had captured the previous year. Cecil teamed up with Melville Rogers, who won the men's title in the same year and held it for the next four, and within months they had been chosen as the pair to become the first representatives of Canada in an official world skating event — the 1924 Olympics at Chamonix, France.

Originally, former Canadian champion Duncan Hodgson of the Montreal Winter Club, and the reigning ladies' champion, Dorothy Jenkins of the Minto Club, Ottawa, were selected to go as well. Marjorie Annable of the Winter Club, and John Machado of the Minto Club, were back-up skaters in case any of the original four had to drop out. In the end, however, only the Toronto pair travelled to France, as the others withdrew. "They have had no opportunity to practice," was the reason. "There has been no ice at Montreal or Ottawa, whereas Toronto has an artificial plant at the Dupont Street Rink."

Cecil continued to practice, and to promote the growth of amateur skating. A society columnist reported:

> "The club will not entertain propositions of a commercial nature, and where admission is charged, the club will accept no remuneration but will expect the proceeds to be used for some local benefit....Among them (the skaters) was Cecil Smith who is only fourteen years of age and has created a considerable sensation with her wonderful performance on ice."

A sensation she was to remain. When she finally set out for the Olympics in early January 1924, accompanied by her mother and sister Maude, she was a fifteen-year-old with the poise and sophistication which come from years of dedication, thousands of lonely hours on the ice, and the experience of performing before expectant and demanding audiences. This, combined with her natural vitality and joy of living, gave her a presence which appealed to both young and old, and provided a bench mark against which future Canadian competitors would be measured in Europe. She made the trip to Europe on the RMS Montcalm along with the rest of the Canadian Olympic team, The Granites, who were representing the country in hockey, and Charlie Gorman, the lone speedskater.

The day before sailing from St. John, New Brunswick, on the 11th of January, the hockey team played an exhibition game against the Charlottetown Abegweits, and during the second interval, Cecil and Melville Rogers gave an exhibition which drew "rounds and rounds of applause."

When the Montcalm docked at Liverpool and Cecil was met by a hoard of reporters and photographers, she realized she was to be honored, recognized and fêted more in Europe than in her home country — a discovery that many Canadian competitors would make in the future. She was an instant success. "Among the 15 Canadian ice champions who have crossed the Atlantic to compete in the Olympic contests at Chamonix, the most striking personality is Miss Cecil Eustace Smith, a demure, fair-haired 15-year-old girl,'' enthused the Daily Sketch. The rest of the British press followed suit, and throughout her stay in Europe Lord Northcliffe's Daily Mail seemed to have reserved a permanent spot on the front page for a photograph of Cecil; by herself, with Melville, with the Canadian or American hockey teams, and with the British bobsled team.

From Liverpool they went to London, then across the English channel on the boat train for Paris, where they skated for one hour only before catching the overnight train to the south of France. Chamonix held the first bitter disappointment of the trip. With only five days to go before the comptetition, the weather had turned warm and made the ice too soft to practice. While the weather turned colder and ice conditions improved over the next couple of days, things only became worse for Cecil. She developed, for the first time in her life, chilblains on both feet so that even strapping on her skates became a mild form of torture. Practice on the ice was reduced drastically to a few hours before the day of the contest.

However, chilblains or not, nothing was going to keep the young Canadian from experiencing all the joys of participating in the Olympics. Competitors mingled freely in the village of Chamonix, enjoying the horse-drawn sleigh rides, scooting down the bobsled run, and feasting on the superb pastries and bowls of coffee in the dozens of small cafés that served as meeting places for the competitors.

The Olympic parade was a casual amble through the main streets, with the hockey and ski teams carrying their equipment and each country represented by a flag, but no written sign to say who was who. The standard bearers were sworn in representing the two hundred and ninety-three competitors, thirteen of whom were women, and the games were on.

Competing in the ladies' singles with Cecil Smith were some of the finest skaters in the world; Herma Plank-Szabo of Austria, twice world champion, Beatrix Loughram of the United States, and the dumpy eleven-year-old wonder girl from Norway, Sonja Henie. On January 29th, the temperature dropped suddenly, icing up the ski runs and producing the toughest possible conditions for cutting school figures. Not only that, on the the day of the competition there was a mix-up in the timings, and Cecil was roused at her hotel in the early morning by a frantic telephone call. With no time to compose herself, she had to hurry over, "benumbed and breakfastless" as one headline read, and appear in front of the seven Olympic judges. As she went, she reviewed in her mind the figures she was about to cut on the ice: inside back double-three, outside rockers, outside change of edge brackets, outside back-three-change-three, outside back-loop-change-loop, and outside forward counters — the whole routine worth a total of 216 points. Then there would be five minutes of free skating, worth only 144 points. In the end, she scored 230.75 points out of the maximum of 360, less than 20 points behind the bronze medalist. All seven judges gave Madame Plank -Szabo first place and the gold. Beatrix Loughran was second, 49 points ahead of her young Canadian opponent, and, finishing in the eighth spot, was Sonja Henie with 203 points, because, "The Swedish child, best free skater, gave a marvelous exhibition, but failed to finish figures." Melville Rogers, favored by some for an outside run at the medals, was less successful than his partner, placing seventh, with 269.82 points out of a possible 432, behind the winner, Gillis Grafstrom of Sweden (367.89 points), and the runner up Willy Boeckl of Austria (359.82 points).

It was in this event that some of the judges displayed the sort of partisanship which has dominated the sport ever since. The Czech judge ranked Josef Silva of Czechoslovakia first, he eventually ended up fourth, and the two Austrian judges placed Boeckl first. The remaining four judges, none of whom was Swedish, voted for Grafstrom.

It was the judges again, who put paid to any hopes Canada had of returning with any kind of medal from the first winter Olympics. When Cecil and Melville skated in the pairs' competition, they drew the most applause, and a number of French newspapers even went to press naming the young Canadians the first pairs' champions. Unbelievably, it took the judges several hours to decide on the winners, and when the results came out, there was considerable consternation among the experts when, instead of coming first, the couple was placed seventh. The Paris edition of the New York Herald said:

> "There was considerable dissatisfaction over the decision of the jury in the fancy skating competi-

tions, not only in the singles but in the couple contests. The greatest surprise over any selections made by the wise jury came after the announcement was made of its placings in the competitions for couples, when the men left out the Canadian pair from its findings."

While Canada's gold medal in the hockey competition delighted most people, Toronto's Evening Telegram expounded on a theme still dear to the hearts of commentators everywhere.

"The events at Chamonix showed that political sportsmanship and political referees are the curse of the Olympic games. Small countries with few entries must have competitors with a big balance over their rivals from the big countries or their trips will be wasted. Canada would not have had the slightest chance of defeating the United States (in hockey) if their superiority had not exceeded the referee's ability to hand the match to the States.

Miss Smith and Rogers, Canada's figure skaters, if not winning, would have been placed higher had Canada's total contribution of entries made them more important in the eyes of the Olympic committee."

But in the end, it was the competition itself which was important — that, and the memories of those who took part. "It was a great honor, and one of the most wonderful experiences of my life," Cecil Smith Hedstrom sparkled sixty years later. "There is something special about competing in the Olympics, win or lose."

Manchester
27 Feby 1924

Cecil Smith won her first international skating medal in Manchester, England in 1924.

5

Ice Flowers

Her first Olympics behind her, Cecil Smith skated exhibitions in Paris and London, where she continued to draw the attention of writers and cameras, then entered her next international event at the Manchester Ice Palace. The field was a small one with only three competitors, but nevertheless, fact and fancy got confused, and the Canadian media managed to make her the silver medalist in a World Championship — a full six years before she was to achieve that distinction. In retrospect, it's easy to see how it happened. Canadians were more concerned with the fate of the hockey team than with fancy skating, which was still considered by some to be a "sissy" sport. After the Olympics, only the occasional paragraph about the competing skaters arrived from Europe via the wire services, with material often re-written from previously published reports. The groundwork was set for a foul-up.

Until 1930, the World Championships for men and women were held in separate centers, and in 1924, the men's and pairs' competitions were in Manchester, England. To fill out the programme, and perhaps add a little glamor, the organizers included a ladies' international event, which today would be called an "invitational." Cecil Smith was invited.

She competed against two Manchester Skating Club members, Ethel Muckelt and Kathleen Shaw. Both had competed at the Olympics, with Ethel winning the bronze medal and Kathleen placing nine points behind Cecil.

The "special correspondent" of the Manchester Guardian

knew his skating, and was not afraid to pass on some of his advice to the competitors.

> "The tracings of all the competitors were good. The difficult loop-change-loop was perhaps the best done of all the figures. The other figures brought out the chief deficiency of all the competitors — lack of style and correct carriage. Miss Smith was the best in this respect. The others would be well-advised to put into practice the rules of the International Skating Union. 'Free foot to be held only a little way from the ice...Arms hanging down easily, like the free foot, they can be used to assist by their movement, but without raising elbow or hand far away from the body.'
> Miss Shaw should practice skating much smaller figures, and thereby gain swing and edge running. Miss Smith's loops were excellently placed, though her forward ones were too large. Miss Muckelt was very strong and went with dash....Miss Smith skated with speed, sureness and good carriage."

Although the dashing Miss Muckelt won the event, Cecil Smith came second, but in the Toronto papers she was mistakenly accorded "second place in world competition" — an error which has been carried down for years on the Wall of Fame at Toronto's Granite Club.

Back home, the young skater who had done so much for Canada and Canadian skating, went into a ceaseless round of carnival appearances in Toronto, Winnipeg, Hamilton, Quebec, and Ottawa. Carnivals attended by the Governor General and Lady Byng of Vimy, carnivals of "surpassing grandeur," carnivals that were "a riot of colour and action," "drew crowds like a hockey final," and "had two full-sized orchestras," carnivals that showed that "Toronto, in spite of its cult of hockey, is not barbarian."

Melville Rogers, who became the leading skater in North America for the next five years, was also one of the stars, and touring professionals like Norval Baptie, Grace Darling, and later, Shipstad and Johnstone, appeared and advanced the growing link with show business.

In competition, a decade-long rivalry was developing between Cecil Smith and Constance Wilson. Constance was to dominate the Canadian skating scene over the years, winning eight Canadian singles' and seven pairs' titles, and four North American singles' and three pairs' titles. It was a record only exceeded by her brother, Montgomery, who won nine Canadian singles' and six pairs' titles, and five North American singles' and three pairs' titles. These are records which will stand permanently in the future Canadian Skating Hall of Fame.

It was Cecil, however, who was to reap higher honors on the world scene, although one incident marred her career. In 1924, Louis Rubenstein, as president of the Canadian Amateur Skating Association, received an invitation to send skaters from the Dominion to the 1925 World Championships in Vienna. "Miss Cecil Smith is particularly mentioned." Unfortunately, the invitation was not accepted, and Cecil lost the opportunity of becoming established in the eyes of the world judges before the final blossoming of Sonja Henie.

While Cecil was at the Chamonix Olympics, Constance won her first Canadian singles' title, but in 1925, at the Rideau rink in Ottawa, she lost it back again to Cecil. However....

> "Both did splendidly in the school figures...and their free skating programmes were equally artistic and were both skated with the acme of grace and proficiency. Some favoured Miss Smith...for the delicate lightness of steps throughout, her airy leaps and her beautiful spins; others thought that Miss Wilson was a shade more finished and that in even-ness and confidence of execution she had a slight advantage..."

The next year Cecil Smith won the Canadian figure skating title for the last time, beating Constance Wilson decisively in the figures, and although in the free skating the rivals came closer, four judges places Cecil Smith first and only one judge gave Constance the top position.

The 1927 singles event was a reverse of the previous year. Both skaters practiced at the Toronto Skating Club, Constance under Gustav Lussi, and Cecil under Paul Wilson, both men having impressive credentials in Europe and the United States. While the rivalry of the girls was reported to be friendly (only prize fighters hurled abuse at one other before meeting), a great deal seemed to be at stake for the coaches. Whenever Mr. Wilson worked on a new routine for Cecil, Mr. Lussi would drop by to see what was going on, and, "....it wouldn't be long before Constance had put some of the elements into her programme," mused Cecil.

But Constance was also concerned with narrowing the gap in the school figures, for which the majority of marks were given. She succeeded to the point that in the championships "her tracings on the ice were remarkable for their symmetry and exactness." In the free skating again, "there seemed to be nothing to choose between them. Both achieved astonishingly difficult figures and skated with wonderful lightness and grace," and reminded one captivated spectator of "Pavlova in her prime, but Pavlova with winged feet and light as a fawn....", probably the first time in print anyone had hinted that the great dancer was heavy-footed.

It was a busy time for the young skaters. Cecil was the first Canadian to win the coveted I.S.U. Gold Medal for the last of eight figures tests, followed closely after by Constance and Montgomery Wilson. She also took up golf, and several years later won the Ontario Ladies' Golf Championship with Maude as runner up. She would win three times and be runner up twice in later events. Meanwhile, after the Canadian finals in Montreal, on February 19th, they returned to Toronto by train to prepare for the North American Championships at the Toronto Skating Club the following weekend.

The men's event was won by Melville Rogers, now skating out of the Minto Club, Ottawa, and the women's by the holder, Beatrix Loughran of the New York Skating Club, who had won the silver medal at the Chamonix Olympics. Constance Wilson was second, and Cecil Smith third. Again it was the figures that decided the result.

But ahead lay the 1928 Olympics in St. Moritz and the World Championships in London, and, in preparation for the trip, Maude and Cecil trained outdoors at Toronto's Varsity Arena. "It was often so chewed up by the hockey skaters that we became very skillful in skating around ruts," said Maude. Nevertheless, the sisters always had a constant crowd of admirers on hand when they practiced, and drew both whistles from the hockey players who stayed behind to watch, and admiration from local fashion writers."'...Skating costumes...of black velvet with broad white ermine collars and deep bell cuffs, and hats to match with turnback brims of white ermine...."

The worldwide interest in winter sports was reflected in the sharp increase of entries for the Olympics — up from 293 to 491. The Canadian entry grew to five; the Smith sisters, Jack Eastwood, and Montgomery and Constance Wilson.

It was an Olympics of dramatic importance for many sports which also underscored the importance of weather conditions. In spite of the high altitude of Switzerland's most glamorous winter resort, an unseasonably warm westerly wind caused a devastating thaw which affected many performances, stopped the events completely for one day during the meeting, and forced the cancellation of the 10,000 meters speed skating event.

Canada won its second gold in hockey, a title it was to retain until 1936, and in figure skating, European eyes were on Gillis Grafstrom and Sonja Henie. Grafstrom, 30, won his third Olympic gold in spite of a badly swollen knee. His smooth, orthodox, and perfectly executed routines appealed to the judges more than the more aggressive performance of reigning world and European champion Willy Boeckl, or Robert von Zeebroeck's spectacular leaps and spins, practiced on the outdoor rinks of his native Belgium. Grafstrom was described by a leading European commentator and judge as "the greatest skating artist of all time, who has raised skating to the level of poetry."

Fifteen-year-old Sonja Henie won the ladies' gold. The year before, she had placed first in the World's in Oslo, but the prize was tainted by the cry of partisanship as three of the five judges were Norwegian. Although the German and Austrian judges both gave first place to Herma Plack-Szabo, the Norwegians all voted for Sonja. The uproar which followed this victory led to the institution of a new rule by the I.S.U. which allowed only one judge per country at future international events.

At the Olympics, however, there was nothing to spoil Sonja's win. She introduced a refreshingly athletic element into her free skating, and was awarded first place by six of the seven judges.

The Canadian hopefuls were not disgraced. Cecil Smith improved her previous Olympic standing to fifth with 32 ordinals, and 2213.75 overall points, and Constance Wilson came just behind her rival with 35 ordinals and 2173 points.

After the Olympics, the skaters parted for a week while the men competed in the Berlin-based World Championships — in the absence of Grafstrom, Boeckl retained his title, and Wilson and Eastwood placed seventh and ninth — then met again in London where the ladies' and pairs' competitions were being held.

It was the biggest skating event to take place in Britain in a quarter of a century, and King George V, Queen Mary, The Duke of York, Viscount Lascelles and Prince Henry all occupied the Royal Box. This Royal presence had one drawback for the skaters, however, as they were not allowed to warm up but had to go straight into their performances. The day before the event Cecil Smith injured her back, and had to withdraw from competition and a special exhibition to be given for the Royal Family, but Sonja Henie and Maribel Vinson performed, and the crowd witnessed the unusual sight of Sonja Henie falling several times. Once she crashed to the ice and slid for fifteen yards, and after completing her performance, she curtsied to the Royal box and skated across to her parents in tears.

The pressure got to Maribel too, but the young Bostonian handled it with more aplomb. After "pirouetting like a ballerina" she unfortunately "overbalanced and sat plump on the ice." Undeterred, she spread her arms, smiled, and bowed her head as if it were part of the act. The King and Queen led the appreciative laughter of the crowd.

In spite of their unrehearsed contact with the ice, the two girls came first and second, respectively, with Constance Wilson coming fourth for Canada, and Jack Eastwood and Maude Smith sixth in the pairs.

The ladies' performances at the Olympics and the World's caused skating critics to revise some of their opinions. "The Field," a newspaper geared to the country gentleman in Britain, said that since the end of the war, the standard of women's skating had risen enormously.

> "It can hardly be denied by anyone who has seen such skaters as the Misses Henie, Burger, Loughran, Vinson, Brunner and Cecil Smith, whose average age is about seventeen, that they are already vastly superior to most of the lady champions of the past. It is probable that they are better even than most of the

best of pre-war men skaters. The size and pace of their compulsory figures are on the masculine scale, their rockers, counters, and brackets are real genuine turns, their loops are pictures of accuracy and control, and their perfect balance enables them to execute even the most of paragraph figures without apparent effort or loss of pace. Few men today can excel these young girls at compulsory figures, and the situation is the same with regard to free skating."

Notably, two Americans and one Canadian were among the top flight skaters of the world in the praised list. The writer indicated that the standard of pairs had also risen because of the improvement in women's skating.

"Formerly it was notorious that frequently the man had to skate down to the level of his partner. This is no longer so. It is really amazing how these young girls from the Continent, America and Canada can have achieved such a pitch of perfection in such a short time."

By the time those comments appeared in print, the young Canadians were back in Canada where the enthusiasm for the performance of Constance Wilson in the world competition was recorded in a poem entitled, "Ice Flower."

"Swanlike in thy realms of pearl,
Tossed by silver clouds of snow;
Like some dainty elfin girl
Dancing in Auroral-glow!
Sway and leap in utmost bliss,
Till thy brittle senses swoon,
And the sun-god's ardent kiss
Ends thy happy, fragile bloom!"

While not quite the stuff of a poet laureate, it did signify the beginning of an era when Ice Flowers would reign supreme.

**Sports cartoon from the Toronto Star Weekly in 1928 featured
Cecil Smith as Canada's top figure skating hope.**

6

Girl in White Boots

In 1930, this light-hearted report appeared in the New York World.

"Two fellows in the lobby of the Hotel Lincoln were amusing themselves yesterday by trying to guess the business or profession of various ones who passed...For instance, one would bet that a scholarly-looking guest was a lawyer or a banker by the manner in which he carried his newspaper...Another guest — a young and attractive girl — was unanimously selected as an actress because she carried a theatrical weekly under her arm... But a dispute arose between the two, about an attractive young woman who suddenly swung gracefully through the lobby...One fellow said she was the secretary to some big banker or businessman, and stuck to it...The second fellow insisted she was an ice skater...That caused the first fellow to howl with laughter...But the other took his guess seriously and begged his friend to go with him over to the clerk...He agreed, and over they went, the one asking the clerk who the girl was who was just turning the corner to take the elevator..."Why, yes, I know her sir," said the clerk, "she is Miss Cecil Smith, Canada's champion lady fancy figure skater."

The reporter was wrong on one fact — Cecil was not Canada's champion. Canadian judges had consistently marked Constance Wilson ahead of her in home-based competition, but at the 1930 World Championships in New York, Cecil was, once again, the darling of the press. Cameramen in search of a glamor picture would sooner or later snap the twenty-one year old, shingle-haired beauty from Toronto. "Daring Darling," alliterated the Daily News in a photo caption.

> "Cecil Smith is the pride of Canada, where she's the queen of fancy ice skaters. She's shown cutting curlicues in world's championship tourney at the Madison Square Garden last night. Her skill and daring on the ice won repeated storms of applause for the Quebec (sic) beauty."

Skating fans, and the have-to-be-seen social elite had been treated to a preview of the World's events at a spectacular carnival at the Gardens a month earlier.

While the world was reeling from the financial collapse of 1929, New York socialites rushed to pay $250 for a box, and $25 for an arena seat, but it was all in a good cause. Inspired by the example of Toronto's carnivals, New York had decided to make the carnival a charity affair and hold it annually.

> "With Madison Square Garden transformed into a rockbound Norwegian coast, New York society donned fantastic costumes, some of which might have startled the natives of Norway...The carnivals has long been bruited about in smart circles. Almost everybody who is anybody had some part in it, and the rest paid, and paid dearly for the privilege of attending...
> The exquisite skating of Sonja Henie, world champion who has earned the title "Pavlova of the Ice" won the most adulation and applause. Miss Henie, a slim blonde girl from Norway, only seventeen, appeared in a costume of gold cloth...and went through whirling spins and turns and intricate dance steps....
> The feature numbers included the Veiling of the Sun,

in which Beatrix Loughran was the golden sun, and
those of the Misses Cecil and Maude Smith of Toronto, Miss Maribel Vinson, and the Dance of the
Bullfighter by Willy Boeckl.
Airplane leaps and spins, very modern and very daring, held the audience breathless as performed by
Norval Baptie and Gladys Lamb, supported by four
couples.''

Only Gillis Grafstrom was missing. A fall on the ice had given
him a concussion, and he was not to appear at the championships
to defend his title. But there was no dearth of bit players to follow
the professionals, and the society of New York, liberally laced with
titled European émigrés, vied with each other for mention in the
social columns.

"Costumed to represent frozen rivers of Russia were
the Princess Nina Caracciolo, Colonel Satar Kahn,
Mme. Theodore Sachno, Theodore Sachno...Baron
V. Juhn von Pushentahl, Miss Gertrude Owen, Ma-
jor John Palmer, Leo Baldwin and Princess
Stephanie Dolgorouky.''

The Roosevelts, the Astors and the Rockefellers were there,
along with "the outstanding representatives of the sports,
theatrical, financial and civic worlds." Skating had been validated
by the right people.
While the elite checked the social columns, the skaters were
back at daily practice, but none were free of the attentions of the
Henie family. Cecil was visited in the arena while she was practicing her figures. "First came Sonja, swathed in furs. Then came
Mother, swathed in furs. Then Papa Henie, with a fur coat and
cigar. Then the brother, with long blond hair, carrying Sonja's
skates, and behind him one of the international judges. Sonja
walked over to my patch to see what my figures were like, but I said
nothing — just smiled."
Cecil could afford to smile, as she had a stylish côup up her
sleeve. "At that time, only professionals wore white skating boots,
while the rest of us wore black or tan. I decided I was going to wear
white boots in the World Championships. Well, my mother was

horrified. She thought it was brash, and the effect on the judges would be too startling, but I did it anyway. Three months later, Sonja was wearing white boots too.''

The championships, the first to include all events at the same site, took place at Madison Square Garden before capacity crowds, February 3rd-5th. The women's event was the focus of attention for both spectators and press.

"They were here at 9 o'clock. Nine o'clock in the morning, the time most of them begin to think about ringing for muffins and marmalade and cafe au lait. They had come in limousines and town cars.

They saw . . . six girls skate geometric designs on thin ice, six girls with suede gloves and ambition to own the good, solid, respectable title of world's champion figure skater.

The Ice Club, reached by an elevator large enough to accommodate a luncheon party of elephants, is somewhere in the upper reaches of Madison Square Garden. Red wicker chairs surround the green cloth partition, dividing the ice people from the nice people.

There, to repeat, at 9 o'clock yesterday morning, were the inspired few to whom figure skating means more than a little . . . Miss Cecil Smith of Toronto, white suede gloves, black velvet with cloche hat to match, skated out. Sonja Henie of Oslo in wine coloured velvet, skated out . . . Maribel Vinson of the United States skated out. Mrs. Constance Wilson Samuel of Toronto skated out. So did Suzanne Davis of Boston and Mollita Brunner of Austria. The audience did not skate out. It smoked, it ate hot chocolate . . .

There was the silence of a cardroom at a men's club as the girls went through their paces (compulsory figures). Sonja wore a rabbit's foot.

She had more showmanship than the others, inspected the ice before each figure, watched Cecil Smith stolidly when the Canadian girl traced, retraced, retraced.''

The skaters were kept in suspense until the end, as the marks were not announced until after the free skating event worth one-third the total number of points. This was held the night after the figures, attended by an audience dressed in evening clothes.

Velvet seemed mandatory for the skaters; Cecil Smith in black trimmed with white fur, Sonja Henie in salmon edged with fawn fur, Maribel Vinson in salmon topped by a black toque, Constance Wilson in gold.

Constance was the first skater to perform, "displaying fine balance in every one of her feats, she seemed to place chief dependence upon swirls and spins. Her back swirl spins were done with much brilliance. She was well-received by the crowd, and gave a sparkling performance."

She was followed by Suzanne Davis and Melitta Brunner, then by Cecil Smith.

> "Miss Smith, who in her school figures had shown a subdued grace that won her the esteem of the critics ...made her bow with a long swan glide, ending with a one foot spiral, and then set off to dance in complete abandon. Afterwards, the beautiful Canadian girl declared that she was startled for a moment as she looked up at the crowded galleries. Then, as the crowd, sensing her wonderful grace and poise began cheering, she set forth to outdo herself. Her performance was received with loud applause."

Sonja Henie skated last and began her four minute performance with a running glide that ended in a daring one foot jump.

> "From this she swung into a flowing waltz...Her forte seemed to be in the more intricate swirls, pivots, and pinwheels...The most sensational of her efforts was her double pinwheel, the formation and execution of which produced the optical illusion of a flaming torch being rapidly turned in the air."

When the results were announced to the 13,000 spectators, Sonja Henie had retained her crown, Cecil Smith was second, and Maribel Vinson, the American hope who had put herself out of

contention for the gold with a bad fall, came third. In the pairs',
Constance and Montgomery Wilson were fourth, Isobel and
Melville Rogers fifth, and Maude Smith and Jack Eastwood
seventh.

Canada had come of age on the international skating stage,
and Cecil Smith, the hockey-playing girl from Toronto, took
home the country's first medal in World competition.

Eighteen-year-old Barbara Ann Scott in Davos, Switzerland.

7

Girl in Emerald Green

While Cecil Smith was earning her silver medal and the plaudits of the press, a fair-haired baby was perfecting her walking technique in Ottawa, already demonstrating the determination and mental-physical co-ordination that was to help her become an accomplished all-round athlete; a tennis and badminton player, golfer, horsewoman, pilot, and... skater.

As she grew older she climbed trees like a monkey and hung by her legs from the branches, learned to swim in two weeks, and became a dedicated and talented pianist. While she helped put her playthings away, she displayed the elements of order and neatness which were to become her trademark.

Watching and encouraging every move was her father, Clyde Scott. He nicknamed her Tinker, but the rest of the world would know her as Barbara Ann.

Lieutenant Scott, of Canada's 2nd "Iron" Battalion, was a veteran of World War I. Severely wounded in both hips, one knee and one eye, he was left for dead on the battlefield of St. Julien in April, 1915. His shattered body was placed on a pile of dead infantrymen awaiting burial behind the German lines, and only rescued when an Alsation medical orderly at a nearby tented field hospital heard his groans several nights later.

Even then, he was thought to have no chance of survival and was placed on a screened-off cot to die. When German surgeons found time to attend to him he was barely breathing, but sheer grit, later manifested in his daughter, rescued him and kept him going.

Although his parents, who thought he'd been killed in action, had already held a memorial service in Perth, Ontario, he fought his way back to life. Finally he was fit enough to be sent to a prisoner-of-war camp and later, for the last months of the war, to internment in Switzerland. There, he fell in love with the peaceful valleys, the mountains, and the orderly manner in which the Swiss lived and farmed. He marvelled at the way the roadmakers tidied up at the end of a day's work, at the neatness of their homes and gardens, and the way they stacked their winter fuel, making patterns out of the different shaded log ends. Although he never returned, this affection was communicated to his daughter by the fireside of their rambling brick home in Sandy Hill. He also imbued his young daughter with his beliefs; that winning and losing weren't important, what really mattered was how you played the game, and that ladies and gentlemen were made and not born. Above all else, Barbara Ann was taught to be a lady.

Her first skating experience, however, wasn't auspicious or even particularly lady-like. At the age of three, she received her first pair of skates, and her mother took her to Dow Lake near Ottawa for her initiation onto the ice. Unfortunately, the skates had the despised double blades, and were not "real skates with boots." Heartbroken and furious, Barbara Ann sat down on the bank and stubbornly refused to put them on. Instead, she spent the afternoon watching a man fish through a hole in the ice.

Over a year passed after the Dow Lake incident, and, determined to get the right sort of skates, she finally wrote to Santa Claus asking for skates with single blades and picks. Christmas Eve found the hopeful letter-writer running a heavy cold and suffering from an ear complaint that would plague her throughout childhood, but a few minutes after the man with the white beard left, she crept out of bed, located the boots and skates, and strapped them onto her tiny feet. When her parents went to her room on Christmas morning and drew back the curtains to let in the thin wintry light, Barbara Ann was asleep with her boots on — one skated foot hanging over the side of the bed.

The Scott income was limited, but what was available went to Barbara Ann. She was enrolled as a member of the prestigious but barn-like Minto Club, the skating home of Melville Rogers. "The walls were so thin that there seemed no protection against the cold, and I felt that I could poke my fingers through," she was to recall.

Within two years, she had exhibited a talent that drew the attention of members and coaches, and her father decided to stretch his resources and hire a tutor to allow even more time for skating. There were conditions, however. She had to agree to keep up her music lessons and maintain the high grades she was already achieving in school.

Her life now settled into a taut routine, centered on the Minto Club. Early morning piano practice, and evening work on her lessons — German, French, Latin and mathematics — bracketed relentless work at the rink. There she honed her skating abilities and her self-control. While her mother sat at the side of the rink wielding the symbols of skating motherdom, a pair of number nine knitting needles, the diminuative Barbara Ann coped with the demands of school figures. Sometimes the big kids raced through the traces she had so laboriously layed down, and sometimes she was knocked over, but she always got up and went carefully on. She only went home when she had successfully completed the required hours of practice, and then it was often with chafed knees and dried tearstains on her cheeks.

Barbara Ann, like her Canadian predecessors, revelled in preparations for club carnivals, in spite of the extra work and late night rehearsals. The Minto Follies was an annual extravaganza that rivalled the performances of the Toronto Skating Club. At age eight, she appeared as the Spirit of the New Year in the Follies, and the Ottawa Journal described her as "the darling of the show." But the same year she recorded an even more significant achievement by earning her bronze medal in figure skating.

For every figure skater, the ultimate goal outside of competition is earning the gold medal, awarded on completion of eight tests of increasing difficulty. Many people spend their entire skating lives trying, and never even getting as far as the sixth test for which a bronze medal is awarded, yet the darling of the Follies received her bronze when she was only eight.

Shortly afterward, she attended the summer skating school in the giant arena built for the 1932 Olympics at Lake Placid. The fact that she was able to skate all year meant she had advantages that her forebears would never have dreamed of, and at nine she passed the test for her silver medal. As a reward her father gave her a gold ring set with three emeralds which had once belonged to Queen Anne. It was to become a lifetime treasure. She originally wore it on her engagement finger to avoid damage from excessive hand-shaking, but by the time she achieved world recognition, she had to switch it to another finger because of persistant rumors of romance.

When she was working for her gold medal, Otto Gold became her coach. She regarded this as propitious, just as she was later to skate for a world medal on Friday the 13th with the number thirteen on her arm. The discipline he imposed at the Minto Club, and at his summer school in Kitchener, never varied and often extended beyond the skating rink. "You will be in bed at nine thirty!", and when the backsliders weren't up to par the next morning, "What were you doing in such-and-such a place at ten o'clock last night when I told you to be in bed?"

One time, Barbara Ann was having trouble with a "three-change-three" which required that the right knee be turned out. After two days of turning the offending knee inwards, Gold ordered her to go home and write out one hundred times, "When doing a three-change-three, I must keep my right knee turned out." With her busy schedule, the youngster felt she was overloaded, and now she had an additional burden. So, her homework done, she scribbled out the hundred lines with a pencil. It didn't matter if Mr. Gold could read it or not — he knew what it said.

The coach took one look at the assignment and said, "Do it again, in pen and ink." He paused, then added, "And neatly!"

It was a lesson she never forgot, and a coaching attitude that years later she had determined was entirely sound. "A teacher must take it for granted that you respect him, or you would be wasting your time taking advice from him."

At aged ten, while the war clouds were gathering over Europe and threatening to spread across the world, she became the youngest Canadian ever to pass the gold medal test. Her coach fixed black eyes on his record-breaking protege. "Now we can begin to learn to skate," he said.

In her first major competition, the Canadian Junior Championship, she came fifth, wearing a dark-green knitted dress her mother had made as she sat at the side of the rink. Barbara Ann regarded the deep emerald of her birthstone as her lucky color, and wore the dress in competition until it was too small for her. Even then she could not be persuaded to throw it away. As an Olympic champion, she still kept her lucky green "competing dress" in her closet at home.

In 1940, still wearing her lucky green, she won the Junior crown. The next year, in the Senior championships, Mary Rose Thacker took the title from Norah McCarthy who was placed third. But the sensation of the championship was Barbara Ann, the diminutive twelve-year-old, who whiled away the long waits in the dressing room practicing ventriloquism with her Charlie McCarthy doll. She was placed second, ahead of the deposed champion, and the adverse comments aroused by her high placement puzzled the young skater. "I couldn't see how I was different from the others. We all did the same work at practice sessions, we all kept strict training, we all gave up the usual companionships and other interests so that we could spend the best hours of the day on the ice."

Her showing in the Senior Championships led to her first appearance in the North American Championships in Philadelphia, but on the morning of her school figures she felt feverish and dizzy. Psychosomatic was not in the vocabulary of the young skater, so she decided she was "just being silly." During her figures the fever increased, alternating with chills, so she slept through the afternoon and evening before returning to the rink for her free skating programme. The judges placed her fifth, and an hour later the doctor diagnosed a case of German measles. After being confined to her room for several days, she was finally smuggled from the hotel, a shawl wrapped around her face, and taken by car on the long haul to Ottawa.

In September of that same year, she suffered the most overwhelming tragedy of her life. Clyde Scott, who had been working around the clock at his wartime duties with the Defence Department, collapsed and died. His young daughter, who had shared his determination and belief in fair play, experienced all the agonies of a broken heart. But the inherited steel core that was hidden under the delicate exterior kept her moving forward on her chosen path to fame. She wanted to prove that she could succeed beyond her father's greatest dreams, and in 1944, a few months before D-Day, fifteen-year-old Barbara Ann won her first Canadian title. She was ready now for her own assault on Europe, and determined it would be successful.

VÄRLDSMÄSTERSKAPEN
i KONSTÅKNING
Stadion ✷ ✷ 13–17 Febr

Världsmästerskapet

1. **Patricia Molony**............... Australien ....
2. **Barbara Annscott** .... Canada ....
3. **Marilyn Ruth Take**............... „ ....
4. **Bridget Shirley Adams** .... England ....
5. **Jeanette Altwegg** .... „ ....
6. **Marion T. Davies**............... „ ....
7. **Daphne Walker** .... „ ....
8. **Jill Linzee** .... „ ....
9. **Barbara Wyatt**............... „ ....
10. **Liisa Helanterä** .... Finland ....

Programme guide for the 1947 World Championships in Stockholm, Sweden. Note the misspelling of Barbara Ann Scott, competitor number two.

8

The Canadian Rose

Barbara Ann was quietly and fiercely determined to win Olympic gold, and occupy the throne last occupied by Sonja Henie. To get there meant losing a normal teenage life, stepping up her practice schedule to a point where it would preclude almost all other activities, and dealing with the loneliness of the superstar. "I was never with teenagers. I would sit in a corner and listen to older people talk, and not participate too much. In fact I was terrified of people my own age."

In 1945, after successfully defending the Canadian title, she became the youngest skater to win the top place in the North American contest ahead of three time champion, Gretchen Merrill of Boston. This victory gave Canada its seventh women's title in the eleven championships since 1923. Connie Wilson had won four, and Mary Rose Thacker two. The New York Herald Tribune said:

> "It was the spectacular display of youthful skating exuberance by Miss Scott which carried her to victory...Little Miss Scott performed three graceful loop jumps in swift succession, and went into the air freely in Salchow and Lutz leaps, varying her display with dizzy spins, all skated with a fast, perfectly balanced pace...and graceful repose."

She took the Canadian title for the third time the following year, and honors began to pour in. She was named the outstanding woman athlete of the year in a national poll of sports writers, and was awarded the Lou Marsh Memorial Trophy as Canada's top athlete. This had never been won by one so young, never by a woman, and never without dissent on the first ballot.

That year too, she parted with her coach of seven years, Otto Gold, and took instruction from a new coach at the Minto Club, Winnipeg-born Sheldon Galbraith "...a wonderfully agreeable man."

She admired her new coach tremendously, both as a skater and a teacher. "I had seen him skate a shadow pair with his brother Murray in the Ice Follies and they made the best men's pair I had ever seen. When he gave an exhibition, the rest of us might as well have stayed at home."

The first time Galbraith and Barbara Ann met on the ice, he made a comment she never forgot. As she was completing a figure which she had traced six times, so perfectly that only one line appeared on the surface, he suddenly said, "You look like a milk bottle."

He was putting into effect his philosophy that you can't teach anyone who doesn't want to be taught. "You have to get control of the situation so that they are willing to make changes. When I started to coach Barbara Ann, I thought I had better make it strong."

With the Olympics looming, she was more than interested in what he had to say. "I knew we were running out of time. I wanted to find out what I had to do so that I wouldn't look like a milk bottle anymore!"

What Galbraith did was elevate her free skating to a new level of gracefulness, built on the solid base of technical perfection she had worked so hard for. "He didn't like anything too artistic. If I did a lovely underarm movement he would take his gloves off, throw them at me and say, 'I want pure skating..no monkey business!'"

Practice sessions now occupied up to eight hours a day on figures and an additional one-and-a-half hours of free skating. One member of the Minto Club estimated that Barbara Ann skated eleven miles a day on her oversize figures alone, but she still found time to put in her daily stint on the piano, and even give occasional recitals.

With the knowledge that the European and World Championships were skated out-of-doors on natural ice, the Governor General, Viscount Alexander, continued the tradition of skating patronage established by his predecessors, and offered the Canadian star the use of the pond at the official residence, Rideau Hall.

Others rallied around as well, to make sure she would be able to compete. A group of her father's friends raised $10,000 to pay for the trip to Davos for the 1947 European Championships, and to Stockholm for her first appearance in the World's competion. Another family friend donated a beaver coat for the sub-zero temperatures of Sweden.

The time finally came to leave, and Barbara Ann flew to England with her mother, Galbraith, and friend Betty Caldwell. She also took Junior, her mascot koala bear, her year-old free skates, and a pair of skates for figures that had been brought from London by Otto Gold when she was eleven. "They rusted easily, were slightly bent, and ground so thin that if I had been any heavier they would have broken under me."

A few months earlier, Barbara Ann had attended her coming-out ball in Ottawa. Now she was about to debut in front of the world.

In Davos, with the connivance of manager Toni Morasini, the Belvedere Hotel became home, and home meant routine and work. For that year, and her return for the World's in 1948, the same room, the same table in the dining room, the same waiter, the same practice space on the giant ice rink. It was a boon to the competitor who valued neatness and precision above all things.

While other tourists and competitors sought out the late night attractions of the small village, Barbara Ann was in bed by 8.30 p.m. and up again at 6.30 a.m. for her balanced breakfast of boiled eggs, cereal and fruit juice. She practiced on the wind-roughened ice, and acclimatized herself to the altitude and the cold.

Galbraith was in constant attendance, assuming the roles of secretary, organizer, press agent and coach. At one point, a dispute with Mrs. Scott over style almost sent him home, but Barbara Ann made the decision, and he stayed.

After three weeks she was ready, physically and mentally, and the crowd was ready for her. On January 31, wearing a white sweater embroidered in red and blue and a matching bonnet on her head, the peaches-and-cream girl became the first North American to win the European Championships. In brilliant sunshine, she skated her six school figures and came in first. Then for the free skating, she drew number seven which she considered lucky, and the whole village turned out, with the thousands of visitors, to see her perform. As she swung into her programme to the music from Coppelia, the crowd began to chant, "Barbarelli! Barbarelli!" She skated on, performing double flips, double loops, and Axels. Long before the judges recorded their verdict, the crowd knew that Canada had produced a champion. When she returned to the hotel, the manager was waiting at the door with a bouquet of seven roses and a handmade card with seven stars.

The introduction to Europe had been accomplished brilliantly. Now it was on to Stockholm, and the freezing conditions of the World Competition.

In spite of the -20° Fahrenheit conditions, Barbara Ann was out in front right from the start. She was encouraged in her school figures by the crowd shouting, "Good! Good! Good!" and once again sporting her "lucky seven" was the only competitor of the morning session to receive no mark lower than five. When she finished, she skated to the dressing room and put her feet on the hot radiator. Her eyes were streaming from the biting wind and she said to her coach almost plaintively, "I couldn't see my traces, and I'm freezing!"

"Your figures were fine, and don't worry about the cold!" he replied. "Think of the judges!" he added. "They're still out there."

Fifteen thousand spectators came to see the free skating, including the disgruntled local pressmen who had been forced by the organizers to pay for their own seats, and who sat clasping the spartan programmes which listed names of competitors and little else.

Concerned about the poor organization of the Swedish Figure Skating Association, they were critical of nearly everything, particularly the judges. In the men's event, they panned the results when Hans Gerschwiler of Switzerland beat out a 17-year-old American, Dick Button. But they had no quarrel with the decision in the ladies' event.

Barbara Ann, cheered on by the crowd, skated to music from Coppelia and Jerome Kern's "Showboat," and gave an even more outstanding performance than at Davos, in spite of the hard ice.

She earned two sixes, perfect marks, and was placed first by eight of the nine judges.

When the winners were announced, the Swedes went mad with enthusiasm — belying their more familiar stolid natures. Although Sweden hadn't dominated the top honors this year as it had in years past, the people were generously behind those they regarded as worthy successors. All the medalists were given armloads of daffodils, flown in from Holland, and when the skaters attempted to leave the ice, thousands of spectators left their seats and blocked the way.

Everyone wanted to get a closer look at Barbara Ann — the Canadian rose who had blossomed in the Nordic winter. After half an hour, with Sheldon Galbraith on one arm and Hans Gerschwiler on the other, she was escorted to a tiny box where the scorekeeper had been sitting. When the crowd attempted to lift the box, the little group dug their toe picks into the ice and headed for the dressing room in the opposite direction.

This near hysteria was only the beginning. Barbara Ann's achievement earned her the plaudits of the world press, the praise of her coach, — "she outskated everyone, including the boys, with the exception of Dick Button," — and of Ulrich Salchow, who wrote:

> "As a class, the ladies' standard was higher than the men's...From the beginning and all through the figures Barbara Ann Scott had the lead and not far behind followed Daphne Walker of England. Barbara's shoulder work made her glide on sharp edges and get good pace through all the figures. She had good luck all the time and she certainly deserved it. The evening show of free skating was brilliant! What the ladies gave was a demonstration of the highest class of skating, gracefulness, courage and good taste. Barbara Ann Scott was the girl of the lucky strike. She combined her difficult programme in an artistic way where her stunts were mixed up in astonishing surprises, all executed in an easy style as if she skated only to have a good time for herself."

Congratulations poured in from all over the world. There was a cable from Viscount Alexander, Governor General, and one from Prime Minister W.L. Mackenzie King, which reflected the feelings of the nation. "Canada is delighted with your well-merited victory. We are tremendously proud of you, and will ever remember the honour you have gained for yourself and for our country in winning the Ladies' World Championship in figure skating. Your perseverance and constant application over years of training will be an enduring example and inspiration to the youth of all lands and to none more than to young Canadians. Warmest congratulations and kindest remembrances."

Barbara Ann was on her way to her heart's desire, an Olympic gold medal, and Canada had its first international Queen of the Ice.

TIME

THE WEEKLY NEWSMAGAZINE

Boris Chaliapin

BARBARA ANN SCOTT
At St. Moritz, double Salchows and open Choctaws.
(*Sport*)

9

Shining Star

The 1948 European Championships took place in Prague halfway through January, followed a month later by the World's in Davos, Switzerland. Sandwiched in between was the Olympics in the winter resort of the smart set — St. Moritz.

Four competitors were invited to represent Canada in all three events — Barbara Ann Scott, Marilyn Ruth Take, Wallace Distelmeyer, and Suzanne Morrow.

There were many critics who thought it would be unwise for Barbara Ann to attempt to defend her European title. A bad marking by the European judges could prejudice her chances in the Olympics, and other Olympic aspirants were avoiding the contest in Prague to preserve their strength. On the continent, there were other critics indulging in the kind of downput remarks usually credited to boxing promoters. One Swiss coach told a newsman that, "Miss Scott is the weakest figure skater to hold a World's championship in many years." Other experts predicted she would fail because most of her training had been done indoors, whereas the Europeans had learned to master the varying conditions of outdoor rinks. Barbara Ann's only response was quick and to the point. "I guess I'd better start becoming the hardy outdoor type," she said, and went to practice, once again, at the Rideau Hall rink. Sheldon Galbraith, after a year spent developing his pupil's showmanship, and skating every one of her programmes alongside her at his summer school in Schumacher, Ontario, was equally unimpressed with the arguments. He firmly believed that Barbara Ann could outskate not only all the European women, but the men as well and he knew that nothing could deter her — not even the unfortunate and humiliating incident of the spring before.

After her stunning and uplifting victory at the 1947 World's competition, her return to Ottawa had been one of the biggest receptions the city had ever seen. Thousands of cheering fans lined the streets trying to catch a brief glimpse of the golden girl. Most had never seen her perform, many had only witnessed a short film clip on the Movietone News, but everyone loved her just the same.

While a thirty-two piece band at the railway station played "Let me Call You Sweetheart," hundreds of children, let out of school for the event, waved autograph books excitedly from behind the guard of honor.

A cream-colored Buick convertible carried the champion to to the Château Laurier and the crowd roared its approval along the way, setting a pattern which would be repeated all across the country, so that cities had to suspend their anti-noise ordinances during Barbara Ann's visits.

At the culmination of the reception, the mayor presented Barbara Ann with the keys to a canary yellow Buick convertible, meant to be a courtesy car, with the license plate 47-U-I. For several weeks, it was the signal to people that the skater was in the vicinity, but before it had even clocked a thousand miles, the car was back in the showroom again — the cause of a raging controversy.

Nowadays, when amateur athletes are paid vast amounts of appearance money, make commercials and then put the profits into trust funds, and receive subsidies from all sides, it is difficult to understand the fuss that arose when a young woman, relying on her family and friends to raise money to send her to competitions, was given the use of a car — with the approval of the Canadian and American Amateur Athletic Union. But fuss there was, started by Avery Brundage, President of the U.S. Olympic Committee, and future president of the International Olympic Committee.

He received a newspaper clipping, referring to the gift of the car, at his home in California, and the fact that other athletes had received cars without losing their amateur status did not seem to faze him. He declared roundly that Barbara Ann had lost her amateur standing on three counts; by accepting the gift of the car, by accepting a gift of jewelry, and by considering a Hollywood contract.

Barbara Ann and her advisors prepared a statement denying the receipt of jewelry and the discussion of a Hollywood contract, then, in tears, she drove to City Hall, and handed her keys back to the mayor. The car, returned to the showroom window and appropriately labelled, was one of the tourist sights of the capitol city for the next year.

Her amateur status secured once more, Barbara Ann tried to forget the needless furor by concentrating on the ever-increasing number of charitable performances, carnivals and exhibitions she had to appear in, and the eight hours of practice needed every day to prepare for the Olympics.

Finally it was time, and the Canadian skating team travelled to Prague for the oldest international skating event in the world — the European Championships. There, in spite of having to practice at 4 a.m. in the pouring rain because the Prague stadium was rented to the public during the day, and in spite of skating the school figures with water rippling over the ice blown by a strong and bitterly cold cross-wind, Barbara Ann dominated the first part of the competition. Later, on ice made uneven by the changing weather conditions, she skated out in front of twelve thousand spectators and swooped into her performance. Seconds later, the music faded and died. Like the champion she was, Barbara Ann simply stopped skating and, without visible signs of stress, waited until the mechanical trouble had been repaired. Then, when the music resumed, she gave a superb performance, earned the highest marks ever given at Prague, and was awarded first place by all seven judges. In the men's event, Dick Button claimed the title, ahead of Hans Gerschwiler, and Edi Rada of Austria, third. North Americans had taken top honors in the European contest and were never invited back.

Barbara Ann, the radiant winner disproving the dire predictions of failure by her critics, completely captured the hearts of the embattled Czechs. Her photograph was printed in local newspapers seventeen times in three days, beating out Rita Hayworth, the red-headed Hollywood bombshell, who had only made the paper eight times during a recent visit.

Her coach made an impression as well, which lasted over the years, and encouraged many European skaters to cross the ocean and attend his summer school. Instead of standing aloof from competing skaters and their trainers, Galbraith went out of his way to communicate with them in spite of language and political barriers. At first his offers of friendship were greated with suspicion, but soon they were welcomed and bonds were formed.

Meanwhile, at St.Moritz, on the slopes of one of the highest valleys in Europe, the snow lay five feet deep — dry and powdery on top and solid beneath. It was ideal for skiing, and a guarantee that the resort would be packed.

Thronging the streets were the rich and not-so-rich, the titled and untitled, many of them heading for the swank Palace Hotel. Celebrity hunters had their work cut out for them keeping tabs on actress Paulette Goddard, Britain's famed jockey Gordon (later Sir Gordon) Richards, ex-King Peter of Yugoslavia, the Marquis of Milford Haven, and a Debrett-like clutch of princes and dukes.

The smart set was out to have fun, and during the evening, their antics often included egging on some dinner-jacketed reveller as he attempted to swing from a chandelier — often with a girl sitting on his shoulders.

While the socialites played their games and prepared to watch the skating from the balconies of The Palace, many of the European skaters, including the British, led an impoverished existence on a ridiculously low expense allowance, and the Canadian team was warned to avoid all signs of ostentation.

Most of the competitors, however, shared a familiar daily routine, lightened only by the beauty of their surroundings; early to bed, careful diet, no alcohol, and, above all, constant practice right up until the moment of performance.

The Olympic parade started at 10 a.m. on Friday, January 30th, outside the elegant Kulm Hotel where the school figures would be performed on the outside rink. With 713 competitors (including 77 women) and over 100 officials and coaches from 28 countries, it was a grand affair when compared to the first parade attended by Cecil Smith and Melville Rogers, but still far removed from the extravaganzas of today.

The Canadian skaters in their navy blue blazers with the red Maple Leaf crest, were led by the team manager, Melville Rogers, and the chaperone, Mrs. Scott, and followed by the Canadian hockey team in RCAF uniforms, destined to win back the Olympic crown lost to Great Britain in 1936. As they continued the friendly stroll down the hill to the official Stadium, beauty was all around them in a virtual winter wonderland.

The oath taken by competitors was unchanged. "We swear we come to the Olympic games...in a chivalrous spirit for the honor of our countries and the glory of sport."

There were those who believed that for many competitors in postwar Europe, this oath had little validity.

One reporter later commented: "In an assembly of feuding factions, whose dogmatic attitude sometimes reduced the Games to a farcical level, it was a pity that some organizations did not settle their domestic disputes at home beforehand, instead of airing their grievances in public while the Olympics were on."

Time magazine, which had made Barbara Ann its cover story, noted a deeper and grimmer game afoot. "For some Iron Curtain countries, like Rumania and Yugoslavia, competition had become almost a matter of life and death: some athletes were nervous about going back home if they didn't perform up to snuff," and wondered if this was to be the last Olympics.

In spite of this bitter note, Barbara Ann tried not to allow anything to disturb her, not even receiving thirteen as her skating number. Also, there were hints of Hollywood tycoons among the spectators — men who could match and better the one million dollar contract signed by Sonja Henie after she won the 1936 Olympics, but for Barbara Ann, the only contract she visualized was with the St. Moritz ice, and that ice was already showing signs of causing problems. The weather in the winter wonderland was warming up, and that didn't bode well.

At seven-thirty on the morning of the scheduled school figures event, twenty-five women competitors, including a sister of Sonja Henie, tramped down to the rink. Waiting for them were judges and referees, some reporters and cameramen, and a sprinkling of spectators.

The temperature was still climbing, and by noon the ice was so soft and water-covered, that after the contestants had completed only one figure, the event was postponed for twenty-four hours.

The next day the skaters mustered at the same time, but the sun still blazed down on the ice, and the judges on hand had to delay skating until the afternoon, and then again until the next day.

Rumors abounded. The event was going to be transferred to Davos, to Zurich, cancelled. Nerves, already taut, were near breaking point for some of the competitors. Barbara Ann kept practicing in one corner of the huge rink while the Poland-Italy hockey game was played, and tried to keep calm. The ice would harden eventually, she and the philosophical Galbraith reasoned, and she had waited so many years for this day that a few hours more wouldn't hurt. Nevertheless, that night she prayed for a drop in the temperature.

Although the ice was not perfect the next day, the event went on. The wear and tear on the participants' nerves was evidenced when Eva Pawlik of Austria made a mistake in one of her figures and burst into tears, but Barbara Ann's determination to produce perfect traces overrode both the poor quality of the surface and outside distractions. While she was skating one of the most difficult figures, a loop-change-loop, a Swiss Air Force plane roared across the rink at rooftop height, throwing its shadow on the ice. Every face was turned up towards the noisome offender, but when Sheldon Galbraith spoke to Barbara Ann about asking for a reskate because of the plane, she just looked at him in puzzlement and asked him what plane he was talking about.

As she moved toward the end of her school figures, cameramen and photographers came within a few feet of her, but she never took her eyes off the incredibly fine lines on the ice. In the end she led with 858.1 points.

Just after dawn the next day, the first hockey game was played in brilliant sunshine, and the second one started at eleven o'clock. The free skating was scheduled for early afternoon and Sheldon Galbraith, although a spectator, was not studying the actions of the hockey players, but the surface on which their skates were moving. He hurried back to the hotel to confer with Barbara Ann, fearful that no matter what the ice-makers tried, the end result would be the same — shale ice. This was a thin covering of quickly frozen ice over an underlying layer of water which gave no solid base for a take-off, and almost no chance for a safe landing. But he also knew that only a third of the huge skating rink in front of the Palace hotel had been boarded off for hockey, and that when the boards were removed, there would be a long strip of ice down one side of the rink where no hockey had been played, and where the dreaded shale would not form after flooding. With little more than an hour before the start of the competition, he and Barbara Ann worked out a variation of her planned programme which could be skated on the narrow surface.

The competition started at one o'clock. It was the kind of day on which, in years to come, sun-seeking skiers would take to the slopes in bikinis. Barbara Ann wore a thin, cream-colored outfit, its lining decorated with the signatures and good wishes of the people who had made it for her in Toronto. Ironically, it was made entirely of fur — to protect her from the kinds of sub-zero temperatures she had suffered the year before.

As she waited in the dressing room, she could hear the applause for skaters who preceded her, including the audience reaction to her friend Eileen Seigh of the United States, whom she had met as a young girl at Lake Placid.

As Eileen skated onto the ice she received the customary welcoming handclap, then the music started, and almost immediately a loud "oh-h-h" rose from the crowd. Barbara Ann wondered what new element Eileen had introduced into her programme. There was another long "oh-h-h," and as the music ended, a third shout and the closing applause. "She's really made an impression," thought Barbara Ann. "I'll have to be good to beat that."

Then the American skater returned to the dressing room — her dress torn and covered with slush, her story grim. The ice, wracked up by the hockey players, was covered with deep ruts hidden by unfrozen water. The shale ice, which was everywhere, had caused her to fall down three times.

Barbara Ann took a deep breath, and as she got up to skate, she touched the golden key of the Toronto Press Club pinned to her sleeve. Here was the moment she had worked toward for thirteen years, had skated over 20,000 hours and 100,000 miles to arrive at. Here was the moment she wished her father could share.

There was a tremendous burst of applause at her appearance, then the stillness of the mountains descended on the crowd. The first bars of Les Patineurs (The Skaters) sounded, and suddenly Barbara Ann was living the most important four minutes of her life on a long narrow strip of ice, after months of preparation on a full surface. One double loop instead of her planned three, but it drew loud applause. Then the double flip which had been Eileen's downfall — the applause grew louder and longer. A double Salchow, another double loop, spins, camels, combination jumps, and a change of tempo. The strong beat of Victor Herbert's

Toyland brought repeats of her earlier jumps, and finally three double Salchows to replace planned double loops.

It was over. A standing ovation, Mrs. Scott in tears, Sheldon Galbraith yelling, "She's won! She's won!"

Then the final announcement.

1. Barbara Ann Scott. Canada. 11 ordinals .166.077 points.
2. Eva Pawlik. Austria. 24 ordinals .157.588 points.
3. Jeannette Altwegg. G. Britain. 28 ordinals 156.166 points.

She had received seven of the nine first place votes — and won the coveted gold medal.

The Canadian hockey players, gold medalists all, rushed onto the ice, hoisted her onto their shoulders, and carried her round the rink to the unceasing and thunderous chant of, "Barbarelli! Barbarelli! Barbarelli!"

The next day, in a snowstorm, she was the first individual Canadian to stand on the winner's rostrum at the Winter Olympic games. "I remembered my father and felt happy, sad and proud, all at the same time."

As the news flashed around the world, Norrie Bowden was working at his engineering books in Toronto, eight-year-old Donald Jackson was in his first season on figure skates, the parents of two young Czech skaters, Otto and Maria Jelenik who had recently given their first public skating performance, were making plans to escape from Prague, Petra Burka, the sturdy two-year-old daughter of the Dutch Ladies' Champion was learning to skate in Amsterdam, Barbara Wagner, a Toronto nine-year-old, was deciding to take skating lessons, and hundreds of young skaters were vowing to emulate the princess from Canada, who would shortly defend her title at the World Championships in Davos.

The old guard of European trainers and judges had been successfully introduced to a new world of excitement on the ice, and Canada had crossed new boundaries on the skating map.

Barbara Ann Scott rehearsing for her professional ice debut in New York City in 1948.

10

In Search of a Picket Fence

Barbara Ann was now confirmed in her stardom with all the trappings. There were telegrams by the score; from the skater she had replaced as Olympic champion, Sonja Henie, from the Governor General, from well-wishers in all parts of Canada, the U.S.A., and Europe. The cable she received from Prime Minister Mackenzie King summed it all up. "From one end of Canada to the other, there is great rejoicing at the high honour you have brought to yourself and to our country."

Almost before she'd had time to absorb the fact that she had won, she was beseiged with requests for autographs, photographs, interviews, money. And constant pleas to turn professional. "I want to get married and live in a house with a white picket fence," she informed an astonished world press. "I want to go to McGill University and take their homemakers course."

"Great Scott!" punned the New York Daily News. "She'd rather cook!" But the same paper set the tone for the world adulation which followed.

> "Beauteous Barbara Ann Scott, Canada's sparkling ballerina on the ice, won the women's figure skating championships ...before 7,000 dazzled admirers, who hailed her performance as superior to Sonja Henie's best as an amateur."

She stopped off in London on the way home, and her whirlwind tour of the British capitol included a measuring session at Madame Tussaud's and a reception at the delighted Canadian Embassy. Her main dissappointment, which she communicated to the press, was that she was too late for the public display of the wedding dress belonging to the young Princess Elizabeth, who had recently married her Prince Philip. Hours after the story appeared in the London papers, she received a personal invitation to visit Buckingham Palace and have a private audience with the Princess herself. Afterward, she went to St. James Palace where she saw room after room of wedding gifts, and of course, the beautiful dress.

The return journey was arduous — a delayed airflight to Gander, diverted to Sydney, Nova Scotia, where crowds of fans had waited for ten hours in sub-zero temperatures.

The plane finally arrived at two o'clock in the morning, and while Sheldon Galbraith and her friend Margaret McGuiness sat in the airport cafeteria eating bacon and eggs, Barbara Ann stood outside in the snow shaking hands with a long line of admirers.

Three hours later at Montreal, she again demonstrated her ability to smile, be attentive, and say the right thing. For the army of newspapermen and newsreel photographers, she was the perfect pick-me-up after an all-night wait.

Her reception in Ottawa was even more tumultuous than a year earlier. Seventy thousand people jammed the streets around Union Station, and stopped all traffic through the center of the city. As she toured the streets in a car strewn with daffodils, more and more people poured out from offices and homes to greet their home-coming queen — the famous skater from that little club down the road.

Soon, the whole country had gone wild. Thousands of little girls sported replicas of the straw hat, with the red poppy sprouting six inches from the crown, that she had worn in the welcoming parade, while department stores struggled to keep up with the demand for the $5.95 Barbara Ann Scott doll, complete with skates and fur-trimmed dress. Exhorbitantly priced skating costumes sold by the thousand.

Within a month of her return, the pressure for her to turn professional mounted and grew. She resisted until friends of her father, who had rallied round to pay her way to Stockholm, finally persuaded her. They helped her set up a foundation which would use a percentage of all her future earnings to aid crippled children, and in June, she announced that she would be giving up her amateur status. Immediately, the city of Ottawa presented her once again with her convertible, which had been sitting and waiting for the past year. Since she was now out of the jurisdiction of the pious Avery Brundage, she was more than happy to accept the Buick, repainted blue, particularly since the license plate had been updated to celebrate the year of her biggest victory and now read 48-U-1.

Unfortunately, she didn't enjoy the move into the gypsy life of the professional skater. Audiences wanted to be amused or startled, but often weren't able to appreciate the finer points of technical skating. "Skating for an audience is so different from skating for judges," she would say. "I always like to put in a double loop just for my own satisfaction, and sometimes there's someone up in the audience who gives a tiny clap, and I know there is a skater somewhere in the crowd."

She had to skate on ever-shrinking surfaces, from the 30' x 40' tank at the Hollywood Ice Revue, to the 24' x 20' tank in Chicago. She had to live out of a suitcase doing five shows every day except Saturday, when she did six — fine agony for a self-professed homebody.

Her typical day consisted of getting up at 8.20 a.m., drinking a glass of juice, going to the theater, putting on heavy makeup and false eyelashes, limbering up wherever there was a space. Then the first performance, newspaper interviews, the second performance, radio interviews, the third performance, answering fan mail before a quick milkshake for lunch. More of the same until midnight, then off with the hated makeup, into some street clothes, over to a local cafe for a hurried meal, back to the hotel, and finally, thankfully, to bed. In the first couple of weeks, she lost over six pounds from her already slender body.

Her first Canadian tour was arranged by Osbourne Colson who also choreographed and directed her performances, and the crowds always demonstrated their great affection. Whenever they came into a town, even if it was only a train stop, the children would be let out of school to see and cheer Barbara Ann.

She kept up this hectic pace for five years, and then, when she was twenty-five, hung up her skates for good. "I still love to see other people do it, but can't go out and skate as well as I used to, and since you can't live in the past, I won't skate at all." The perfectionism which had started her career also ended it.

But skating did lead her to the domesticity she had always longed for. She had already met and fallen in love with the revue's publicity director, Tom King, and in 1955 they married and moved to Chicago, leaving Barbara Ann Scott, the skater, to live on in memory. Her achievements have been described and praised by many. Three views help explain the impact she had on the skating world.

Maribel Vinson, who competed against Cecil Smith, was nine times U.S. champion, and a North American single's and pairs' champion. "Every other skater has good days and off days...but Barbara Ann was different. For instance, she would go out one day and do a dozen or more school figures. If she went out the next day or the day after and did these same figures, the traces would not vary by as much as an eight of an inch. She would do them precisely the same way as she did them the last time. She was undoubtedly the most consistent woman skater of all time."

Sheldon Galbraith, coach and trainer said, "She was a perfectionist with phenomenal balance, who could place school figures wherever she wanted, as often as she wanted. In free skating she could outskate most of the men of her time. She became the sweetheart of the world because she was a refreshing young beauty on the sporting scene, and we had endured so many years of war, and things that weren't pleasant to talk about. Now, all countries could get behind her and she would never disappoint them — she was truly their champion. If Barbara Ann were skating today, she would still be able to demonstrate her determination and skill — the qualities that put her at the top in the first place."

Barbara Ann has her own explanation. "The world was kind and took an interest, and in Canada, people were proud because it was the first time a champion had come back to this country. Before, the titles had always stayed in Europe. I don't think I was magical — just the little girl from Ottawa."

The little girl who brought back the gold.

SYMBOL of EMPIRE

P.T.O.

Programme for the Sixth Annual Skating Carnival in St.
Catherines, Ontario in 1945 which featured Suzanne Morrow
and Norris Bowden.

11

Shiver Down the Spine

The next Canadian skaters to gain international recognition appeared, at first, to be an unlikely combination. Norris Bowden was an engineering student, and Frances Dafoe a dress designer. The catalyst was Sheldon Galbraith, new professional coach at the Toronto Skating Club, who saw in the logical engineer and the artistic designer, a unique partnership able to interpret his own feeling for showmanship.

Bowden had first appeared in the Canadian Championships at the Winnipeg Winter Club in 1942 where he came last. Three years later, however, he teamed with Suzanne Morrow to win the junior pairs' title, and in 1947, while Wallace Distelmeyer and Morrow won the senior pairs' and dance waltz titles, he became the Canadian men's champion. In 1948, he declined an invitation to compete in the Olympics so he could continue his studies.

His fiancée, Frances Dafoe, had been skating since she was eight "to use up some of my excess energies," and had no major competitive ambitions. A couple of broken ankles stopped her for two years, but carnivals rebuilt her enthusiasm. It was after she and Bowden became engaged that they started skating together and decided it would be fun to go into the dance events.

The fun paid off, and in 1950 and '51 they won the Canadian waltzing title. In 1952, when the first World's dancing event was held, Canada abandoned the subdivisions of the dance championship, and Dafoe and Bowden won the first of the new all-round dance titles along with their first Canadian pairs' title. By then they were moving into world contention, and pairs became their sole concern.

From the beginning the skating relationship was stormy. Two young people, each with a very determined mind and strong character, were not only engaged to be married, but trying to sustain a working relationship of artistic harmony. The skating world witnessed the flare-ups on the ice under the pressure of competition, and the on-and-off engagement. The couple had a difficult time financially, with very little assistance from the Canadian Figure Skating Association which didn't think they had much of a chance, but they always managed to keep going because their coach convinced them that they had a great future.

A contemporary writer noted: "Like most teams of talent, Dafoe and Bowden have their squabbles. Most of them stem from interpretation of the music to which they skate. Galbraith is the final court of appeal. They both accept his decision without dispute."

The coach had an incredible influence on them, not just as figure skaters, but as human beings. He put together their programmes, then made sure they had the stamina to go through with them by seeing that they were properly conditioned and eating the right things. They admired him greatly, but Galbraith took a more pragmatic approach. "The Olympic pairs' winners in 1948 only had three jumps. After nine years of war and its aftermath, the Europeans didn't have the quality of development of the North American skaters. It was an easy thing to put Dafoe and Bowden together in a pair that would be up front."

They first competed in Olympic competition at the Oslo games in 1952, where they were placed fifth. The gold medal went to the German husband and wife team, Ria and Paul Falk "whose precision-timing in lifts and skillful shadow jumps and spins was quite unusual."

In the World's at Paris they were fourth, and Canada listed six people in the top ten for the first time. Suzanne Morrow was fourth, Marlene Smith, the Canadian champion, seventh, Vera Smith tenth, and Peter Firstbrook seventh as well.

The Canadian pair impressed the judges, including Canada's Donald Gilchrist. "We developed a whole series of new lifts and new moves in our programme. When we first went to Europe people thought it was tremendously acrobatic, and we were criticized for being too athletic.''

Undeterred, they continued to strive for originality over the following year. They practiced outdoors as well as in, carving out a style that was to put Canada solidly in the forefront of world pairs' skating, and Bowden started and finished each day with fifty pushups to prepare his arms, legs and shoulder muscles for the new lifts.

In February 1953, they competed at the World Championships in Davos, and came second behind Jennifer and John Nicks of Great Britain. Four other Canadian skaters were in the top ten, but in the singles, it was the year of the United States. Hayes Alan Jenkins took over the men's crown from five-time champion Dick Button, with the luckless James Grogan, second twice to Button, coming second again. Tenley Albright, sixth in her first appearance in 1951 and a no-show in 1952, swept up the women's title with firsts from all seven judges.

The following year saw both skaters polishing their programme — they won their second Canadian pairs' title as well as the North American title — and building the basis for their future careers. Bowden had completed his engineering degree, obtained his Master's in commerce, then gone into insurance, while Frances was concentrating on expanding her business as a fashion designer, and producing the costumes for them both to wear at the 1954 World Championships in Oslo.

Like many skaters, before and since, they felt the pressure of economics. Frances put the cost of her outfits, two for practice and two for competition, at six hundred dollars. Boots cost eighty dollars a pair, and blades thirty-five. Bowden estimated that the cost of getting to the championships was six thousand dollars, which he regarded as a modest investment compared to the almost thirty-six thousand lavished on the training of the American, Hayes Jenkins.

A nine-strong Canadian team travelled to Oslo for the February competition, plus Melville Rogers as judge, coach Sheldon Galbraith, and Frannie's father, a Toronto surgeon and brother to the Dr. Dafoe of Dionne quintuplets fame.

Galbraith quickly introduced his pair to the outdoor skating rink where sub-zero temperatures rivalled those Barbara Ann had faced in Stockholm seven years before. In spite of their conditioning, the Toronto couple was concerned at the effect the temperature would have on their performance.

As they left the dressing room to perform, Frannie noticed a thermometer hanging outside. "I wonder what the temperature is," she said as she headed over to look. "No, you don't!" said Galbraith, and blocked her view. He didn't want her to think cold, but Frannie didn't need anything to tell her how freezing it was on the rink.

"The ice was so incredibly hard that our skates squeaked, and we felt as if we were skating on glue. Since we couldn't wear gloves, our hands froze and we couldn't feel anything — particularly on the lifts."

In spite of this, their performance was so fine that five of the seven judges placed them first, making Dafoe and Bowden the first Canadian pair to win the World Championship.

A prominent British critic said the couple had introduced a new trend in pair skating. "The main thing....is that this Canadian pair are such excellent skaters and have a wonderful sense of music and artistic presentation, combined with precision and style of classical purity."

Once again, Canada's national anthem rang out over the winners' podium — sounding even sweeter after a six-year absence — and the couple was overcome with emotion. "The greatest moment for any athlete is to stand there and hear your anthem played and know that the flag is going up behind you," said Frannie.

"It's not just the medal. It's the fact that you're representing your country — that the flag is over your head, and you put it there." Norrie explained it simply. "It sends a shiver up and down your spine."

After the inevitable exhibition tour in Europe, the champions returned to a decidedly lukewarm reception in their own country. It seemed as if no one outside of the skating community cared whether Canada had produced the best pair skaters in the world or not. Sports writer, Bob Hesketh, railed at the disinterest.

"Canadians are notorious for taking their champions for granted....skating should be the number one Canadian talent. Bowden and Dafoe received sufficient recognition that they were twice written-up in Time magazine. Yet on their return home, after winning the title, a very high government official turned to an associate at an inadequate reception, and demanded, 'What is it these people did?' Such ignorance, if not unusual, is not excusable.''

The lack of enthusiasm extended, sadly, to the other seven competitors — every one of whom had placed in the top ten. If the same results had been obtained in tennis, Canada would have dominated Wimbledon, Rolande Garros, and Forest Hills. Charles Snelling was seventh in the world at his first attempt, Peter Dunfield eighth, Douglas Court tenth, and Barbara Gratton, the Canadian champion, was fourth, two ordinals away from a medal at her first attempt.

If the Canadian public hadn't gone wild at having all this success on the doorstep, knowledgeable people in skating circles were certainly sitting up and taking notice. International judges knew that the Canadian competitors meant business — that they would be coming back and going after the top spots.

As world champions, soon to be defending their title, Dafoe and Bowden continued training, giving much of their spare time to fund-raising events and carnivals. It seemed they were always on the go, but the benefits outweighed the hectic routine as Frances was later to realize. ''The training a skater receives lasts a lifetime, because it develops a strength of will and a tenacity of purpose which can be applied to almost any endeavor. To be a figure skating champion, you have to be a perfectionist, which is something that never leaves you. It is a tremendous training for life.''

That training was to be severely tested over the next two years. The 1954 World Championships were held in Vienna, and the Canadians experienced their third version of outdoor skating — in a blizzard. ''After each pair skated, the ice had to be scraped,'' said Frannie. ''There was nowhere to put the accumulation of snow, and the rink got smaller and smaller. As we skated, the snow built up under our blades so that we didn't have a pure run.''

They tied Sissy Schwarz and Kurt Oppelt of Austria with 17 1/2 ordinals, but only four judges nominated the Austrians for first place, whereas five, including the American and Canadian judges, placed Dafoe and Bowden first, causing them to win the medal by .06 points — the closest margin ever recorded in a world competition. The Viennese papers were furious. Austrian Karl Schäfer, seven-time world champion, said the Austrian pair did more difficult and brilliant figures and were not given full point value for them by the judges. The communist newspaper Der Abend headlined its story, ''Scandal in the Figure Skating Championships.'' It said the Austrians ''are nevertheless the real world champions'' and claimed that a hail of snowballs had landed on the U.S. judge in protest. But although the Austrian press was critical of the judging, the country's inbred love of the sport, developed so long ago in Vienna by Jackson Haines, ensured massive coverage of the championships and recognition of the winners' unique qualities. Dafoe and Bowden discovered that wherever they went in Europe, they were recognized and identified by name – a welcome change from their anonymity at home.

The conditions the skaters had contended with also received wide comment. Presse said: ''An icy wind swept over the ice rink and hampered the skaters in performing difficult school figures. The lightweights had a particularly hard time, and it was not always easy to execute a difficult figure properly.'' Neue Wiener Tageszeitung didn't think that the wind and cold were anything to get excited about. Under the heading, ''Wind spoiled fun for covered ice rink skaters,'' the correspondent took the opportunity to indulge in a ''we're tougher than you'' homily.

> ''The North Americans were despairing. Civilisation
> — nobody can deny it — entails certain signs of
> degeneration. In the western world ice skating has
> turned into something that is done in heated and air-
> conditioned hall rinks. Ice skaters, therefore, are
> more like hot house plants than winter sportsmen. In
> the rough winter air, the enthusiasm of the
> Americans wilted away, and they did not feel so
> much like showing their high class skating. When
> gusts of wind swept over the ice during the perfor-
> mance of the second school figures the boys, who are
> used to drawing their circles without interference,
> were desperate. On the other hand the Central Euro-
> pean open air ice rink skaters, put up quite well with
> the unsatisfactory conditions.''

Nevertheless, the ''despairing'' Americans took the first three

Barbara Gratton and Sheldon Galbraith at Canadian Championships, Oshawa, 1952.

Hayes Alan Jenkins and Barbara Gratton were named King and Queen of the Ice at Lake Placid in 1954.

Frances Dafoe and Norris Bowden competing in Oslo, 1954 .

Frances Dafoe and Norris Bowden receive congratulations from Marianne and Laszlo Nagy of Hungary, after winning World title in Vienna in a snowstorm in 1955. Sissy Schwartz and Kurt Oppelt of Austria are on the right *(below)*.

Norris Bowden led the Canadian team in the 1956 Olympic parade.

The Olympic stadium, Cortina, Italy, 1956.

The Canadian Olympic skating team 1956. Left to right: Norris Bowden, Frances Dafoe, Sheldon Galbraith (coach), Barbara Wagner, Bob Paul, Carole Jane Pachl, Ralph McReath (manager and judge), Anne Johnson, Charles Snelling.

**Norris Bowden and Frances Dafoe retired from competition in 1956
but skated in their club carnival.**

Robert Paul and Barbara Wagner after turning professional in 1960 *(above)*.

Wendy Griner received silver medal at Prague, 1962 *(right)*.

Robert Paul, Sheldon Galbraith and Barbara Wagner at 1958 World Championships in Paris *(below)*.

Sheldon Galbraith and summer school pupils study training film. Top, Charles Snelling and Robert Paul. Center, Carol Heiss (World and Olympic champion), Barbara Wagner and Ann Johnson.

Maria Jelinek, 13, and Otto 15, at 1955 Canadian Junior Championships in Toronto *(right).*

Maria and Otto Jelinek in Ice Capades *(below).*

medals in the men's singles, with Hayes Alan Jenkins gaining first place in school figures from eight of the nine judges. His fourteen-year-old brother David was placed third behind Ronald Robertson. Two other hothouse plants, Tenley Albright and Carol Heiss, were placed first and second in the women's event. All of the Canadians, despairing or not, placed in the top ten in their events.

Eddie Scholdan, the bouncy Viennese trainer of Hayes Jenkins, had watched his young pupil attempt to complete the figures in a raging gale and shrugged. "Ice skating today is a gamble," he had said, but years would pass before the "degenerate" specimens of North American civilization would be permitted to skate indoors.

**Norris Bowden and Frances Dafoe rehearsing for the World
Championships at Davos, Switzerland in 1953.**

12

A Matter of Judgment

Judging at international skating competitions has never been totally without bias. In fact there are enough cases on record to demonstrate gross partisanship. Even at their most efficient, judges are human (although some skaters find that hard to believe) with all the subjective frailities which that implies. Competitors have long railed at the perfidy of those who sit in judgment over their performances.

At the 1908 Olympics, Nicolai Panin of Russia, with two first-place votes for compulsory figures, withdrew in protest when Ulrich Salchow of Sweden was given three. Panin, who earlier in the year had inflicted Salchow's first defeat in six years, claimed the judging was stacked. In 1920, Magda Julin was awarded the Olympic title without a first place vote. The British judge voted for Phyllis Johnson of Britain, who ended up fourth. The Norwegian judge placed the two Norwegian competitors first and second, although all the other judges placed them last.

More recently, Canada's Garry Beacom made headlines when he kicked the boards in protest at what he thought was low marking of his figures during the 1984 Olympics at Sarajevo. Norburt Schramm of West Germany skated off the ice and withdrew from the competition for similar reasons.

However much the judging system with its complicated scoring formulas is adjusted, the human element cannot be eliminated, although it could be somewhat reduced by the use of modern technology and video playbacks, by adopting the professional system of marking individual elements instead of the whole performance, and by putting judges at different locations on the rink instead of in a row like sitting ducks, waiting to be sniped at by armchair and ringside critics. But whatever the improvement, nationalism and subjectivity will end up tipping the scales.

There are those in the know who believe that this inevitably leads to behind-the-scenes lobbying for votes. "I will give my first place to X, if you will support Y." Only an outstanding performance by a major contender can override the deals, and if there are political divisions, sometimes even that won't work. It seems that judges, particularly at the international level, have to know not only their skating, but also their fellow judges. They have to be diplomats as well as politicians.

It was with these thoughts in mind that Norris Bowden and Frances Dafoe felt nervous just before the 1956 Olympics in Cortina, Italy, and the World Competition shortly after in Garmisch, Germany, when it was announced that Donald Gilchrist, the original judge/team manager for the skating team, had been replaced by Ralph McCreath — a judge not yet blooded in the European arena. They expressed their concerns to the Canadian Figure Skating Association, and asked that a second judge accompany the team — preferably Gilchrist himself. They felt his experience and assistance would benefit all members of the team.

They were told that the Olympic body would not accept a second official, and, no, the Association was not prepared to ask if it would reconsider. So the competitors went directly to the Olympic committee, which maintained that they had absolutely no objection to the Canadians having a second official as long as the C.F.S.A. appointed him. They added that since they had no additional funds, they would not be able to pay his expenses if the Association did decide to send him.

Norris and Frances passed this information on to the president of the Association, and said that if it didn't have the necessary funds, the competitors would try to raise money by private subscription. The next thing they knew, the president informed them that he had polled the members of the executive himself and they had decided a second official was not needed. The skaters were given no opportunity to present their case.

During the training period in the fall, the competitors were contacted by the president and threatened with removal from the team if the appointed judge should resign his position. Then things got worse when the president took it upon himself to contact several team members and make tape recordings of their phone conversations. These recordings were not limited to the competitors, but included parents as well. Finally, just before departure, Dafoe and Bowden were called in and told they had to sign a statement saying they would not contact, cajole or try to influence any of the European judges, or in any way jeopardize the position of the C.F.S.A. while in Europe. This document was to be put in a safety deposit box and on their return, if their conduct had been exemplary, it would be destroyed in the presence of the senior pair. Refusing to be intimidated, they did not sign.

Norris and Frances, along with other members of the skating team, asked to depart early so they could train abroad and become acclimatized to the altitude. Their request was refused even though Canada's other winter teams, like the ski and hockey teams, were training in Europe already. Finally, the International Figure Skating Union intervened and made it possible for them to leave and practice in Cortina. Frances said later, "I think Norris and I were the first skaters, other than Barbara Ann, who understood the value of training at an altitude and the effects it has on the body. My father was a doctor, and he went to great lengths to study every possible difficulty. This was very useful to us, and in fact, I think we knew more than the hockey players did, and at Cortina, Sheldon Galbraith shared that information with the hockey coach."

So off they all went, along with the team manager and sole judge Mr. Ralph McCreath, a three-time Canadian champion. For Frances and Norris it would be their last trip to compete, as they had already decided that, no matter what happened, they were going to retire from skating after the World's and devote their time to their careers and to judging.

The 1956 Winter Olympics at Cortina d'Ampezzo, Italy, was the first of the stage-managed extravaganzas that now delight television audiences all over the world, and practically impoverish the host country. In a magnificent setting with the Italian Dolomites as a backdrop to the newly built 2.2 million dollar Olympic stadium, thirteen thousand expectant onlookers waited for the arrival of the Olympic flame, and millions of television viewers watched the ceremonies live for the first time.

The torch had been carried five hundred miles in relay from the ruined Temple of Jupiter in Rome, and handed over to Italian speed skater Guido Caroli for the final lap. He provided the only flaw in the magnificent ceremonies when he tripped on some microphone wires and fell in front of the box from which Italian President Giovanni Gronchi had recently delivered his welcoming speech. Somehow the unfortunate man held on to the torch, completed the circuit, and lit the flame. Then, the tiny Italian skier Juliana Minuzzo took the Olympic oath on behalf of the 924 competitors.

The games were the most colorful and lavish ever mounted, and were subsidized by profits from the national soccer pools, with the gate money from the 157,000 admission tickets repaying only a portion of the $9,000,000 promotional costs. But as the first internationally televised Winter Olympics, the world-wide publicity brought substantial commercial benefits to Italy, and established Cortina as a major winter sports center.

The Canadian competitors, clad in blue three-quarter-length coats with fur collars and alouette toques to match, were led into the stadium by Norris Bowden. The skating team included Frances Dafoe, Barbara Wagner and Bob Paul, Anne Johnston, Charles Snelling, all from Toronto, and Carole Paschl from Ottawa, coach Sheldon Galbraith and Ralph McCreath. As they marched, their toques bobbing cheerfully, they received an ovation from the crowd. "Canada! Canada! Canada!"

Hopes were high for Olympic gold. The Canadian media, true to form, had made wild predictions of success without having first studied the field. Carole Pachl was touted as a possible winner, without, apparently, taking into consideration the talents of reigning champion Tenley Albright, who had been placed first by all nine judges at the World Competition in 1955. Galbraith attempted to tone down the euphoria. "Carole has the experience and the ability, but the toughest thing in the Olympics is to dethrone a champion." The Canadians certainly had the edge in the pairs, but even the most ardent patriot should have known that the Olympic crown was not going to be handed over on a platter.

Galbraith was cautious in his statements. "Frances and Norris are the world champs, and right now they are the best they have ever been."

Team manager McCreath was more optimistic, and told a

Toronto newspaper they should win easily. "They have experience, the most intricate programme content I have ever seen, plus polish that no other pair has shown in practice. I cannot see any other pair coming close to our champions." Later, after judging their performance at the games, he would tell them it had been the first time he had actually seen them skate in three years.

In the end, the winners depended on the choice of the judges. The Canadian pair skated as they never had before. "When you are competing you are not competing to win, but competing against your own standard. If you know that the presentation you have just completed is the very best that you can do, then you are satisfied," said Frances. And they were satisfied they had skated a good programme but for one small flaw at the end of their performance, when Frances faltered on a lift and did not end exactly with the music.

They finished ahead of their Austrian rivals Sissy Schwartz and Kurt Oppelt with 101.9 points to 101.8. In the stands, Maribel Vinson, coach of the new Olympic champion Tenley Albright, had done her own markings and placed the Canadians first. Now the system of declaring winners, unique to skating, came into operation. Both pairs received four first-place votes, but the Austrians were awarded five seconds and the Canadians four seconds and one third. If they had just received one more second placing, they would have won the title because of their higher points score.

They described the second-place finish as the biggest letdown of their lives. "The most disappointing moment is when you know you have done the best you could possibly ever do, and it hasn't been recognized. We wanted that gold medal so badly." The decision was not a popular one, but it had been a bad week all-round for the judges. Earlier in the pairs' competition, twelve-year-old Marika Kilius and seventeen-year-old Lazlo Nagy of Germany had received tremendous applause from the packed stands. Their poor marks started an unprecedented demonstration as the disgruntled crowd, already at the end of their endurance, threw oranges at the judges and referee until the ice became littered with fruit, buns, bottles and other creative debris. Wagner and Paul, waiting to make their Olympic debut, were forced to return to their dressing rooms until the ice was cleared and the crowds quieted down. They were eventually placed sixth.

The controversy that centered around the pairs' event continued on to the World's at Garmisch-Partenkirchen, Germany, where Dafoe and Bowden were to defend their world title.

On the Thursday preceding the closing ceremonies, McCreath had discussed with the team what accommodations would be necessary in Garmisch, and assured the members that everything would be attended to. He then left on the Saturday for Rome, while the rest of the team went to Germany without him. Frances and Norris gave an exhibition performance at the closing ceremonies, but the necessary arrangements for the music and practice ice had to be made for them by the Americans, due to the absence of a Canadian official.

When the team arrived in Garmisch at midnight, they found that they had been directed to the wrong hotel, and when they finally got to the hotel where they were supposed to be booked, the hotel management stated that they had no information on reservations or expected arrival. It was not until two days later that a wire was received by the hotel.

At last it was time for the pairs' competition, with the reigning world champions, Dafoe and Bowden, pitted against the new Olympic gold medalists, Schwarz and Oppelt. The Munich Abendzeitung reported the performance.

> "Frances Dafoe and Norris Bowden were the true world champions of the evening. They were a musical dream poured onto the ice with magnificent double Axel Paulsens, and double Ritterbergers, and strong expressive lifts. The whole arena was thrilled with excitement, and the spectators roared their delight. They were certain they were watching the world champions. The pair thanked them with an aristocratic bow, and the crowd cheered them right to the dressing room."

Now it was the judges' turn to speak the last word and pay the Canadians their due. But it was not to be. Dafoe and Bowden lost their world title to the Austrian team by one ordinal. Five judges placed Schwarz and Oppelt first, three placed them second and the Canadian judge third. The defenders received four firsts, four seconds and a third. The Canadian judge voted them a first, but the American judge gave them his second place vote. The third came from the Austrian judge. Once more Frances and Norris had been edged out of top spot, but this time the storm in the European press was on behalf of the Canadian pair. The Munich Abendzeitung went so far as to call it a false decision.

> "If a few weeks ago the Canadians and the Viennese pair were of the same standard at Cortina, this time Schwarz and Oppelt were nowhere near the precise performance of the Canadians. But not only the Austrian judge was responsible for this regrettable lapse of human objectivity. The Czechoslovak and Italian judges also obviously marked (the Canadians) down. International experts in Garmisch-Partenkirchen are today talking about a new figure skating scandal. Schwarz and Oppelt certainly had good content with lots of pleasant moves, but the exhibition was not as clean as in Cortina, or as sovereign. They were out of balance in spins and the flow from one movement to another was imperfect. There was no ecstatic enjoyment in watching them, but their marks were very high. The Austrian judge gave 5.8 twice, while later he gave the Canadians 5.5 which provoked booing from the crowd."

The Garmisch-Partenkirchen Tagblatt wrote that the Austrian pair were not as smooth and sure as they had been at Cortina, but the judges had marked them higher.

> "The Canadians took the audience by storm. The precision of their performance, the sure quick jumps of the Canadian girl, the incredible tempo and flow of their combinations...But the judges thought otherwise. They decided for Schwarz and Oppelt by a fraction of a point. Even if Dafoe and Bowden did not quite deserve to win at Cortina, last night they earned first place without a doubt."

In the rest of the competition, Snelling had earned a creditable fourth behind the indomitable American trio, Jenkins, Robertson and Jenkins, Wagner and Paul placed fifth, and Anne Johnston ninth. Lindis and Jeffrey Johnston, the Canadian dance champions, who, in 1955, had placed eleventh as the country's first dance representatives in world competition, improved their standing to ninth in the world.

While the younger members still had dreams of challenges to be met, Dafoe and Bowden's dream had been snatched away from them, and the memory of their last competition had been tarnished by the circumstances surrounding the tour.

When they arrived back home, controversy continued to dog their heels. Although the couple had announced their intention to retire before they left for Europe, organizers of the Canadian Championships in Galt, Ontario, thought they would surely be skating in the competition to defend their Canadian title. But Dafoe and Bowden declined so that Wagner and Paul would have a good chance of winning and increasing their standing in international competition the following year.

They found they had to deal with rumors — about getting married, turning professional and having a beef with the C.F.S.A. Bowden scotched the first two, and was cautiously conciliatory about the third.

"Sure we have a beef with the Association concerning the judges Canada should send over to the Olympics — but skaters are always having beefs with the Association," he told the Globe and Mail.

Frances was more outspoken, mentioning some of the real faults they felt existed in international competition. "Norris and I told the C.F.S.A. about these situations, but they just patted us on the heads and told us to forget it. Everybody just pussyfooted around."

The comments did not sit well with the skating establishment, and even less welcome was a twenty-two-hundred word report on the Olympic and World Competitions prepared by Bowden and submitted to the C.F.S.A. "in the hope that some things may be learned from it and thus benefit our skaters for future competition."

The report ended with a list of observations:

1. Training conditions in the fall were most unsatisfactory due to the constant high tension existing and the ever present threat of expulsion from the team.
2. The use of tape recorders in recording telephone conversa-

tions of amateur skaters, especially minors, is questionable. The writer would like to know for what purpose these records were made.

3. The uncompromising attitude of the president of the Association in his dealings with the competitors leaves a lot to be desired.

4. The attempts to get signed documents from the competitors is not new; the writer has been confronted with it since 1953 and was unfortunately coerced into signing at that time.

5. Conditional acceptance on a team is not too satisfactory for it differentiates between team members and can cause unforseen problems. This was evident in 1953 when Suzanne Morrow represented Canada in the World Championships in Davos. On her return to Canada she found that it would mean losing a year at college for her to remain in training and compete in the Canadian championships. She elected to complete her studies and was subsequently required by the C.F.S.A. to refund the plane fare they had given her for her overseas trip.

6. Whether the best interests of the team were considered in selecting a judge who, by his own admission, had not been too interested in skating of late as witnessed by not having seen the Canadian world champion pair skate for three years though they were members of the same club and gave numerous exhibitions, is questionable.

7. The Olympic rules permit a country to have three entries in every event and most countries availed themselves of this opportunity. Canada's original team comprised only one in two events and two in the third event. This meant that the pair of Wagner and Paul were to be excluded — they won points for Canada this year. A more realistic outlook on the quality of the skaters available might prove more satisfactory and pre-empt the possibility of Canada leaving point winners sitting at home.

8. It is open to discussion whether it might be wise, in an Olympic year when there is so much at stake, to send an official who is familiar with World and Olympic competitions, as well as one who is going over for the first time. It is unfair to ask one man to judge all three events, four in World's competitions and manage a team properly while trying to acquaint and ingratiate himself with an organization he has never seen before. It is a two-man job. Though Canada had entries in the Dance competition, she

had no judge overseas who was eligible to judge.

10. If the duties of the team manager were laid down, and understood by all, he would not be left open to any unjust criticism.

11. It is difficult enough to properly train oneself for competition, giving up limitless amounts of time, and, needless to say, investing a considerable sum of money, without having any additional problems to confront. Assistance-not hindrance-is what the competitors wish, and possibly this can be accomplished in the future by exchanging ideas, and working closer together on a more amicable basis.''

The memorandum was submitted to the C.F.S.A., but not accepted. In these days of sophisticated protest, Bowden would probably have called a press conference, supported by other skaters, and brought his concerns into the open. In 1956, he saw it solely as a skating problem, and addressed his concerns to the community he felt would be most concerned — the skating clubs. Adding one more expense to a career which had already cost many thousands of dollars, he had his report copied and mailed to over two hundred affiliated clubs. The Association responded with immediate retribution.

Although Dafoe and Bowden had already announced their intention to retire and not turn professional, both skaters did want to give something back to the sport which had played such a big part in their lives. They wanted to become international judges, a process that usually takes up to ten years, but quietly and without fanfare or publicity, Canada's first world pairs' champions were suspended 'sine die' from judging for over five years. Frances was punished equally, although the preamble to the memorandum said "any opinions expressed are purely those of the writer" and it was signed R. Norris Bowden.

Today, many of the improvements in competitions which they fought for have been implemented, and are now accepted by young skaters without question. Both Dafoe and Bowden are happily married, to other people, and both have achieved their goals to become international judges. And if they don't have the memory of going out on gold, perhaps it rewards them even more to know that their loss eventually brought so many gains to the skaters who came after them.

SPORTS ILLUSTRATED

DECEMBER 15, 1958

America's National Sports Weekly

25 CENTS
$7.50 A YEAR

PERFECTIONISTS ON ICE

World Pair Champions
Barbara Wagner and Bob Paul

13

An Unlikely Pair

The pairing on the ice of a pretty, vivacious, thirteen-year-old girl, and a bespecled, introverted, fourteen-year-old boy was unlikely enough when they were both the same height, but when the girl remained five-foot-one, and the boy shot up another twelve inches, the combination became almost as unusual as their spiralling talent.

The girl, Barbara Wagner, had never thought seriously about skating until she was eleven, when she joined the University Skating Club in Toronto and won the club's annual achievement award in the first year. Not long after, she made a commitment to the sport by moving to the Toronto Skating Club for instruction from Sheldon Galbraith.

The first major test of that commitment came when her parents enrolled her in the summer school where Barbara Ann Scott had trained, and where top skaters from around the world were flocking to discover the secret of Canadian skating success, in the mining town of Schumacher.

The Wagners travelled the five hundred miles north of Toronto to a small frame house that was to be Barbara's billet during her first extended stay away from home. Standing in the doorway of the neat old-fashioned bedroom she had been assigned, she was assailed by the stomach butterflies that were to become so much a part of her competitive future and clutched her skates tightly. "Remember this," said her father. "If you back out now, you'll probably be backing out of things for the rest of your life." Barbara stayed, and cemented the first blocks in her skating career.

The boy, Robert Paul, received his first pair of skates when he was eight, and as soon as he learned to cross a rink without falling, he realized he had found the way to fulfill his dreams. He, too, was only twelve when he first met Galbraith, and had already made up his mind what he wanted to do. When Galbraith asked him what his ambitions as a skater were, he replied that he'd like to be an Olympic champion someday.

Galbraith put these two young skaters together in 1952, not to create a pair necessarily, but to develop their individual skills. Robert had turned into a strong skater, good on figures, but his free skating was somewhat inhibited. Barbara, on the other hand, showed a wonderful abandon in her free skating but wasn't taking a long enough stride, and Galbraith thought that by pairing them off, she would be forced to lenghten her stride, and Bob would learn to let himself go. The experiment worked, and by 1953, it was even beginning to pay off competitively. The couple came third in the junior championships, and Galbraith began to regard them seriously as a team. The following year they won the Canadian junior title, and in 1955, they were runners-up to Dafoe and Bowden in the senior event, and accompanied them to the World Championships in Oslo. "We were their little shadows," said Wagner. "We ate, slept, and breathed their names." But the breakthrough year was 1956 when, after respectable placings in the Olympics (sixth) and the World's (fifth) they won the Canadian title vacated by their mentors.

The door was open, and they skated right through. In the last three weeks of February 1957, they won the North American, the Canadian, and the World titles — one right after the other.

That year, the World Championships, held in Colorado Springs, gave Canada its best results to date in world competition. Geraldine Fenton and William McLachlan of Hamilton, Canadian and North American dance champions, earned Canada's first world medal in dance competition when they were placed second to June Markham and Courtney Jones of Great Britain. Charles Snelling, in his fourth year as Canadian champion, moved up to third place in the world, and young Donald Jackson was seventh. Only the women's event failed to produce a medal, but two Canadians were placed in the top ten — Carole Jane Paschl was fourth, and Karen Dixon, tenth.

As for Wagner and Paul, a mismatched pair of singles skaters seeking to improve their individual talents — they had become a team whose combined strength was greater than the sum of its parts. This was underlined a year later in Paris, when they defended their title for the first time and eight of the nine judges placed them first. Then, on their post-championship tour of Budapest, Berlin, Bratislava, Prague and Warsaw, they noticed they were being studied closely, not only by the enthusiastic audiences, but by other coaches and skaters as well. . . . imitation being the sincerest form of flattery, and a sure sign of success.

They were recognized everywhere, and became known affectionately as Bob and Barbara instead of the more usual Wagner and Paul. In Bratislava, at an exhibition performance, that affection flared into admiration and one of the most memorable moments of their careers.

The indoor stadium was packed for a gala evening of skating, but the people were perfectly still during the performance, watching with expert eyes the North American showmanship they had heard so much about. When the Canadian couple concluded their programme, there was a silence — then, in the tradition of pleased European audiences, rhythmic clapping, calling for more. When the applause for the last repeat died down, thousands of candles and matches were lit in the usual Bratislavian tradition of appreciation. The performers on the ice were stunned by the beauty of this mini-torchlight salute, until, suddenly, the flames all over the stadium grew bigger and bigger. For a moment, Bob and Barbara thought the whole place was burning down, then they realized what had happened. The audience had decided that matches and candles just weren't enough for the brilliance of the skating they had just seen, so they had set fire to their programmes instead, in an unforgettable flaming tribute to excellence.

When the pair returned home, there was another flame on their minds — the flame that would be burning at the Olympics in 1960. To prepare for their assault on the gold, they withdrew from school, and while their peers headed for cottage country and a relaxing summer, they went north to Schumacher and eight-hour practice days with Sheldon Galbraith.

Winter found them back in Toronto again, but this time at a different club. The historic Toronto Skating Club had merged with the even older Toronto Cricket Club and the Toronto Curling

Club, creating a ménage a trois which couldn't seem to come up with a name. Finally, the toss of a coin decided the pecking order, and the establishment, built on the grounds of the Cricket Club on the outskirts of the city, became the Toronto Cricket, Skating and Curling Club — a tongue-twister destined to bedevil future television commentators.

In the new Swedish modern building, the young Olympic-hopefuls lived by a rigid and exhausting daily schedule. Practice started each morning at eleven o'clock, but even before that, they spent hours taping, timing, and listening to music that might be worked into their developing programmes. Barbara took on the additional task of designing the six costumes they each needed for a season of competition, carefully co-ordinated to minimize the difference in their heights.

Then, onto the ice for a fifteen-minute warm-up, individually and then together, gradually working into lifts and spins executed to new music taped by Bob. Sometimes they would devise half-a-dozen routines and reject them all. After the experimental work, they would return to their competition tape, working, working, working on the five-minute programme they hoped would win them a third world medal and propel them to an Olympic gold.

At twelve sharp, Galbraith arrived in his inevitable duffle coat and navy blue cap, carrying an 8 m.m. camera and a projector. This remarkable man, whose influence extended far beyond skating with his many students, used two things to great advantage in coaching — dramatic flair, and learning by seeing. The showbusiness part came from years spent skating professionally in the United States and Canada, and the learning by seeing came from his time in the Navy. During World War II, he taught young pilots to fly by making good use of film, and as a coach, he taught young skaters how to fly as well, without the help of a plane. Often, he would use the same principles of aerodynamics to help create the illusion of graceful weightlessness in his earthbound students, and he insisted that they study their own movements to learn best how to improve. Over the years, he took thousands of feet of film, watching and reviewing the day's work every afternoon with his "team." His methods produced many champions, but he also had his share of disappointments. In 1954, Barbara Gratton was Canadian champion and fourth in the World's. Galbraith had great hopes for her. "She could have been one of the greatest champions

Canada had ever produced," he was to say later. Shortly before her international win, however, her father died, and she was forced to give up her skating, leaving the rest of the story incomplete. Galbraith's hopes were centered on others, and particularly Wagner and Paul.

After his arrival in the morning, he would spend an hour with Bob and Barbara studying the moves they had been working on and recommending improvements. They knew they were getting better, but couldn't help feeling the pressure of having to protect their position at the top from the others who were also improving, and coming on fast.

After lunch, eaten at their respective homes to save money, they would return at three o'clock for more practice and another session with their coach until it was finally time to call it a day, at least as far as the ice was concerned. Then home to listen to music, skating it through in their heads, thinking about each stroke of the skate, imagining every lift. Dates were rare. There was little time for a social life — skating was a tough taskmaster. Anyway, it was important to rest and sleep: to recover from the strenuous day and prepare for the hundreds ahead just like it.

Their different temperaments often produced moments of tension, but usually they would just turn their backs and skate away, rather than say something they might regret later. Their personalities also affected their training and balanced things out in an important way. Bob was diligent about their practice sessions well ahead of a competition and kept Barbara going during this period, then, when the pressure increased and Bob tensed up and started to go downhill, Barbara would get a surge of energy which would carry them both along.

As with Dafoe and Bowden, there were constant rumors of romance between the two of them, but this time the speculations were completely without substance. When Bob and Barbara weren't skating, they kept their lives very separate, and although they gave the impression on the ice that they were in love, it was just an illusion.

If the will to succeed had been strong, the desire to stay successful was total. With two world titles behind them, the competitive pressures piled up and drove them to even more wearying practice sessions, but they had the support to keep them going. "It takes a whole family to make a skater," Barbara said. "The luck of the champion is being born at the right time to make the Olympic games in a peak period. It is being born to the kind of parents who will dedicate their lives to the furthering of their child, and it is having the right kind of coach.''

Were they being driven? ''The better a team gets the more it seems to rely on your help,'' says Galbraith. ''They seem to want you to drive them. With such a demanding timetable, the inevitable tensions of a partnership were bound to surface, but the youngsters had matured, not only in their skating, but in their way of handling personal problems.'' They had also realized that they needed one another to get to the end of the road.

Nineteen-fifty-nine saw the World Championships back at Colorado Springs, Colorado, which one cynic put down to the handsome gifts awarded to officials during the previous hosting. Certainly this time, there was no lack of Western hospitality. The competitors, judges and officials were given cowpoke oufits, complete with genuine Stetsons, for the motorcade to the city Hall. There, they met the Governor, became honorary citizens of the State of Colorado, received deeds to square-foot portions of Pike's Peak, and were introduced to the cowboy star Rex Allen, who arrived dressed in a satin magenta outfit ''oozing baubles, bangles and beads.''

Other activities included a sumptuous banquet with top class entertainment, many private parties given by the Broadmoor Skating Club members, and a tour of the U.S. Air Force Academy accompanied by the Commandant's wife, a former figure skating champion.

Most important, however, were the championships themselves, which confirmed Wagner and Paul as the most dominant pairs' skaters in the world since the prewar combination of Maxi Herber and Ernst Baier of Germany. All nine judges placed them first, in spite of four minor errors in a difficult and varied programme.

On succeeding nights, Wagner and Paul skated exhibition numbers to ''One Fine Day'' from Madame Butterfly, and the Tommy Dorsey arrangement of ''Song of India.'' ''Those two exhibition pair routines really drove the message home to any disbelievers that the Wagner and Paul pair are without peer today, and will be for some time,'' said the team report.

Canada was going to be well-represented in future international competitions, but most significantly, Wagner and Paul had become firm favorites to retain their world title the following year and capture Canada's first Olympic pairs gold medal.

Barbara Wagner and Bob Paul, four-times World Champions and 1960 Olympic Gold Medalists.

14

Star Dust

The 1960 Winter Olympics was a fairy story come to life. In the face of keen competition from three well-established European resorts, Squaw Valley, an empty, scarcely-known Californian site where everything had to be built from scratch, had won the International Olympic Committee vote and been transformed into a perfect home for all the competitions.

A deciding factor in the choice of the location was its compactness. Except for the cross-country ski courses seventeen miles away on the McKinney Creek, all the other venues were within short walking distance. Sometimes it was possible to watch speed skating, figure skating, ice hockey, downhill skiing and ski jumping from the same spot — a visual miracle unequaled anywhere else in the world.

What was known as the pageantry committee was headed by Walt Disney, who supervised all the ceremonial arrangements and created a winter wonderland fantasia that staggered even the sceptics. The fairy tale aspect even extended to the weather. Before the games, weeks of rain, which had threatened to wash away the ski courses, had been followed by an overload of snow and wind that would have devastated the planned Hollywood-style opening featuring Vice-President Richard Nixon. Then, with only fifteen minutes to go before the ceremonies were to start, the skies cleared, the sun shone, and the weather stayed perfect for the next eleven days. Many believed that it had all been stage-managed by Disney, whose own chalet stood on a hill overlooking the resort.

The number of competitors was down by nearly three hundred from the '56 Olympics mainly because the European teams had done some pruning; first, to reduce the cost of travel, and, second, because no bobsled or tobogganning runs had been built, the only real complaints. But the friendly spirit which took hold of both spectators and competitors made up for any deficiencies. This was exemplified when the American hockey team was playing the Canadian favorites, who were expected to win easily. The Russians suggested to the Americans that they breath oxygen during the second interval to alleviate some of the distress caused by the 6,230 foot altitude. The tip paid off handsomely, and the United States went on to win the title with a 2-1 upset. Even the media seemed to enjoy the event, and there were few, if any, who suggested that this would be the last Olympics.

Canada's figure skating team was the strongest ever sent to an Olympic event and, under the tutelage of Sheldon Galbraith, presented the best opportunity of producing a gold medal since Barbara Ann Scott had skated in 1948. As well as Wagner and Paul, who, at 21 and 22, were the oldsters of the team, there were: Maria and Otto Jelinek from Oakville Skating Club, runners-up in the North American's and twice third in the world, Donald Jackson from Oshawa, who, at 18 had become Canadian champion and North American champion in 1959, and runner-up in the World's, Sandra Tewkesbury from Chatham, winner of the Canadian Olympic trials, and, sadly, killed in an accident shortly after the games, Wendy Griner, Canadian Junior champion, at the games to watch and learn, and Donald Macpherson from the Stratford Skating Club, Canadian Junior champion.

The team was strong, youthful and full of promise. Suddenly, skating, which someone had once described as the pastime of martyrs, had become news, and predictions of victory appeared in print and on the air.

The Jelinek's coach, former Canadian waltz champion Bruce Hyland, voiced the feelings of many when he said, "Canada will have the two best pairs in the Olympics. It's just a question of which will win."

But for Wagner and Paul, there was no such certainty. "Never did I believe we were going to win automatically," said Barbara. "It was a fight to the end."

Both skaters had witnessed the failure of world champions

Dafoe and Bowden to capture the Olympic title in Cortina, and remembered their own unnerving experience when they were sent back to the dressing room while the ice was cleared of debris thrown at the judges. They had reached these Olympics with no scandal, no major upsets, always being very careful to avoid anything that could cast a shadow on their amateur status. The memory of Avery Brundage and Barbara Ann's yellow convertible was always present. In an interview with the Globe and Mail, Bob Paul even refused to identify the make of the old car he drove to skating practice in case someone considered this an endorsement.

Now all they had to worry about was their performance. Just before they had come down to California, they had tightened up, and their skating had lost its spontaneity and become very mechanical. "There were so many people believing in us," said Barbara. "They said, 'Oh, you've won three championships — there's no way you're going to lose.' Well, of course there was a way we were going to lose. If we fell flat on our faces, we were going to lose."

At ten in the morning of February 19th, after a short spell of jogging on the spot and a few well-chosen words of encouragement from Galbraith, Bob Paul and Barbara Wagner took to the ice at Squaw Valley.

The ultimate test was at hand. Years of practice, requiring patience, courage and countless precious hours, all had to be condensed into one five-minute programme. There would be no second chance, no fumbled ball which could be recovered and converted into a scoring opportunity. Just one bad mistake, and all that effort would be erased.

There was a pause while they waited for their music. Oddly enough, in the midst of the most sophisticated outdoor rink the sporting world had ever seen, the music for the skaters' programmes was played on a record player which stood on a small table, totally unprotected, watched over by a single official. At last there was the unmistakable sound of needle hitting vinyl, then the opening bars of the Kalmen Memory sounded out and the pair skated off. They had practiced this routine over five hundred times; rapid skating for two-and-a-half minutes, slow and sensitive for one minute, then a fast-paced finish. They circled the rink once, building up speed, then performed a difficult lift, skated again in unison, and broke off to perform individual Axels.

They were showbusiness personified: nothing could come between them and a gold medal now. Suddenly, there was the magnified sound of a needle careening across the surface of a record — then silence. As a hum of speculation swept through the crowd, the skaters stopped and looked at Sheldon Galbraith in his Hudson's Bay coat, holding the inevitable movie camera. Beside him, the official in charge of the music was leaning over the record player. Several minutes passed, then an announcement on the audio system stated baldly, "Wagner and Paul will restart their programme."

"It was probably the best thing that could have happened to us," said Barbara later. "We'd gone around the rink a couple of times and had a chance to loosen up." So, off they went again and, miraculously, skated their best performance ever. Then it was over. As the judges held up their marks, Sheldon Galbraith jumped to his feet in excitement. The pair had been awarded first place by all seven judges, and would receive the gold medal. Relief came first for the new Olympic champions, and then came the tears.

At the beginning of March, with the daffodils starting to bloom in the Vancouver parks, the World Championships took place in Canada for the first time. Before an unashamedly nationalistic audience, the best pairs' skaters the world had ever seen produced a flawless performance, capturing their fourth and last world title. The decision to turn professional was not long coming.

They joined the Ice Capades, and quickly learned the rigors of the touring pro skater, but unlike Barbara Ann Scott, they both enjoyed the world of show business and loved the glamor of the ice shows. They worked long, hard hours with performances twelve times a week, but "there were great compensations. Seeing the country, visiting museums and art galleries in every little town we went to, meeting so many wonderful people on tour . . . One year at Christmas we wrote out over 1,200 Christmas cards, and received more."

After four years Barbara married an American skater with the show, Jimmie Grogan, and Canada's most successful skating team broke up after an eleven-year partnership. They continued their quest for excellence in skating, Barbara as a teaching professional, and Bob as a choreographer for some of America's greatest skaters like Peggy Fleming, Dorothy Hamill and Linda Fratianne.

About their success and the golden moment of Olympic triumph, Bob remembers, "It was a long, hard haul, but that's what any competitive sport is. The timing was very good for us, and we've always been appreciative of that."

"We were lucky kids — we really were," Barbara says. "When you think of all the people who strive for the top and the few who ever succeed, looking back now we say, 'that was really lucky....'"

The one piece of luck — the stopped music which allowed them to relax into their greatest victory — remained a mystery until many weeks after the games were over. Then they discovered that Sheldon Galbraith, while moving over to get a better position for his filming, had lightly and innocently brushed against the unsecured table holding the record player. It was a twist of fate no one could have foreseen — the light dusting of luck on the foundation of hard work which always adds extra glitter to the winners.

Ihr Ziel – die Goldmedaille

Die Geschwister Maria und Otto Jelinek, kanadisches Meisterpaar im Eiskunstlauf, placierten sich letztes Jahr an den Weltmeisterschaften im dritten Rang und hoffen nun, wie viele andere Paare, auf die goldene Medaille bei den Weltmeisterschaften 1959 in Colorado Springs. Inzwischen absolvieren sie in Davos ein strenges Training. Beachten Sie unseren Beitrag über das sympathische Geschwisterpaar auf Seiten 16/17.
(Farbaufnahme: H. P. Roth/Pelican)

Nr. **5**

XXXV. Jahrgang
29. Januar 1959
Erscheint Donnerstags
Ringier & Co AG
Zofingen (Schweiz)

70 Rp.

Deutschland DM –.80
Frankreich ffr. 70.—
Italien Lire 130.—
Oesterreich Sch. 5.50

**Maria and Otto Jelenik occupied the cover of a Swiss magazine
while training in Davos, Switzerland.**

15

The Return Home

When Barbara Ann Scott completed her medal-winning performance in the St. Moritz Olympics in 1948, two of the most enthusiastic people in the audience were Henry and Jarmilla Jelinek, wealthy Czechoslovakians who had travelled to every winter Olympics since their marriage in 1930. For them, and for thousands of others in postwar Europe, the arrival of Barbara Ann and North American skating showmanship brought light into a shadowy Europe suffering from the ravages of war.

The Jelineks had always been interested in figure skating and had encouraged their children to take up the sport, but it was Barbara Ann's performance which started them thinking how wonderful it would be to have a world champion in the Jelinek family.

They started with Frank, the eldest, and followed with Richard, but neither boy showed any aptitude at all for cutting neat patterns on the ice. Little Otto and Maria, however, had formed a natural partnership against the world, and were exhibiting a great deal of talent on their skates. A year earlier, the tiny twosome, Otto six, and Maria four, had given their first public performance in a carnival at the Winter Garden in Prague. Arriving on the ice before their scheduled time, they discovered there was no music, so Otto sang to provide the rhythm. Their debut was greeted with delighted applause, but never could their ambitious parents have drafted the scenario which was to produce a fairy tale ending for the Jelineks, and give them not one world champion but two.

Their life in Europe in 1948, however, was becoming more like a bad dream than a fairy tale. Czechoslovakia had been one of the first casualties of the war — its new-born democracy crushed under the iron heel of the "master race." Then freedom had come along with the Russians, and the Czechs were once again struggling to build an independent nation. But even while the Jelineks were at the Olympics, the Communists, backed by the U.S.S.R., had taken over the country.

Henry Jelinek had been a victim of Nazi persecution during the Occupation, and he knew only too well the ramifications of a totalitarian government. He knew too, that the family business would be impounded and that at the very best he would become a servant of the state.

When he returned home to Prague his worst fears were confirmed. The cork factory now belonged to the workers, but because of his experience and world-wide contacts, he would graciously be allowed to remain as manager. The five children, Frank, Richard, Henry Jr., Otto, and Maria, were to be brought up under the new Stalinist regime, their futures out of his hands.

It seemed that it was time for the Jelineks to leave their beloved country, so while the world was still celebrating the victory of the blonde superskater from Ottawa, they planned their escape — first to Switzerland, and ultimately to a hundred-year-old home in Oakville, Ontario.

Their move to Canada provided an impetus for the family skating ambitions, and dreams of a champion, in a completely back-handed way. In the late forties, the expression "D.P." was still used freely in North America, meaning "Displaced Person." Anyone from Europe who looked, spoke or dressed differently, could be dismissed with this short and convenient expression of opprobrium, and that included the Jelineks. For the parents, who were busy building a new business and a new life for their children, it was not too painful, but for the younger ones, just entering the Canadian school system, being excluded was puzzling and hurtful. They desperately wanted acceptance, and decided that doing well in sport was the way to get it. Otto and Maria found the achievement they sought in their continuing enthusiasm for skating, and progressed from the natural rink on the front lawn to the loneliness of early morning practice sessions at the Oakville Skating Club under the direction of Bruce Hyland. More training followed after school, with Maria becoming adept at changing into her skating outfit in the back of the family car.

After two years, Hyland decided to enter them in their first competition in Ottawa, which they won. It was the first step on the road which would eventually lead them back to Prague.

The road wound through Lake Placid, where the whole family sojourned in the summers while the skating prodigies studied under Gustav Lussi, former coach to Dick Button, and around to the Canadian Junior championships in 1955, where Otto and Maria entered the record books for the first time, and became Canadian Junior Pairs' champions — without opponents. At the last minute, the only other pair entered were forced to default because of injury, so the Jelineks, fourteen and twelve, skated their programme, not to compete, but to earn sufficient points to justify being granted the title. They also got a write-up.

> "Not only is the Jelineks' skating of high technical exactitude and brilliance, but on the ice they make a fascinating picture with their unaffected youthfulness. Otto is a most engaging boy, bright-faced and alert in body. His sister, Maria, skating with her pigtails merry-go-rounding gaily in her self-created breeze, is a vision right out of fairy tale books."

They had their first opportunity to compete in a senior competition when they were invited to the World Championships in Vienna in 1955, but since that city was still under the rule of a four-power commission, one of which was Russian, Papa Jelinek was not prepared to expose his escapee children to the risk. They were sorely disappointed and frustrated at seeing their path to the top blocked by something out of their control, but the next day they returned to the practice rink to put in the hours and miles on ice that would give them the opportunity to try again. As they were trailing the established top pair, Wagner and Paul, they had the advantage of a constant local talent to aim at.

In 1957, they made their first trip to a World's event in Colorado Springs, and were placed third. They maintained their standing in Paris in 1958, but after missing the Canadian and North American Championships in favor of spending time training in

Switzerland, dropped back a place in the 1959 World Championships, again in Colorado Springs.

For the young skaters, it was a disastrous competition. "Their
programme was jammed full of content — too much, in fact. On
this particular night, they had a bad time of it — they should do
better next year," wrote the team manager. They could not afford
to do worse. They had four major falls, and the death spiral concluded with Maria being dragged across the ice on her back.

In spite of this, it was the following year at the Squaw Valley
Olympics that they suffered the biggest disappointment of their
careers, when they failed to get into the medal ranking, placing
fourth behind Wagner and Paul, Marika Kilius and Hans-Jurgen
Baumler of Germany, and Nancy and Ronald Ludington of the
United States. The Jelineks were shocked, as they felt they had
skated one of the best performances to date, but swallowed their
disappointment, and went immediately back into more practice —
preparing for the World's in Vancouver.

There they placed second, and with the current champions
turning pro, they were on a springboard that could lead to the title
itself. The only problem was that the next World Championships
were going to be held in Prague.

The young couple were full of enthusiasm, but their father
thought it was too dangerous, and was adamant in his refusal to let
them go, for although the Jelineks regarded themselves as totally
Canadian, to the government in Prague they were still
Czechoslovakian. Papa consulted the Minister of Foreign Affairs
in Ottawa, and was told that the only way out of the predicament
would be if the communist authorities in Prague released Maria
and Otto from their citizenship.

The International Skating Union in Davos was called in, and
with twenty-eight affiliated skating associations behind them, approached the Czech government through the Czechoslovakian
skating body with an ultimatum. Either the Jelineks would be
given safe passage in and out of Prague, or the World Championships would be moved to another site. Desperate for foreign cur-
rency and already heavily committed to staging the championships, the authorities began to waver. Then a few days after the
deadline when the event was about to be transferred to Dortmund,
Germany, they gave in, albeit reluctantly, and the Jelineks travelled to Montreal where they received the documents releasing them

from Czechoslovak citizenship. The way was now clear for them to go to the World's, but first they had to compete in the North American Championships in Philadelphia, and once again, a block was thrown in their way. The day before the competition, they were practicing a difficult lift which had Otto rotating Maria above his head. Suddenly, his feet slipped, and he fell backwards with Maria tumbling into a heap on top of him. As the ambulance rushed them to the hospital — Otto unconscious, Maria staunching the flow of blood from a deep gash on her leg — it seemed that they might not need the guarantee of a safe return to Prague after all.

But the fates hadn't reckoned on the stubbornness of the Jelineks. Although Otto had remained unconcious for over forty-five minutes, he left the hospital with stitches in his head, determined to compete the next day. Maria, in spite of the stiffness of her leg, backed him up.

They stuck together, they skated together, and they won together — with four 5.9s and one perfect mark of 6. The headline in the Philadelphia Daily News read, "Plucky Jelineks Steal the Skate Show." Jack McKinney, who covered the event, wrote:

> "Otto Jelineks's hair had been carefully combed to hide the three stitch wound on his scalp, but a broad strip of bandage was plainly visible on Maria Jelinek's right thigh.
>
> Injured in a serious practice spill, the comely brother-and-sister team from Oakville, Ontario, had chosen to ignore the advice of the physician who treated them. Devotees of their refined sport would call this 'pluck'. In the baser sports it's known as guts.
>
> Twenty minutes later, the Arena was ringing in tribute to the Jelinek's exciting program of spins, multiple turns, difficult lifts and unison figurations. There would be other champions in the Awards Ceremonies — Laurence Owen of the United States for the Ladies' Singles, Donald Jackson of Toronto for the Men's Singles, Canada's Virginia Thompson and William McLachlan for the Dance Championship. But this day belonged to the Jelineks. . . . Otto bears a three inch scar over his right brow, a perma-

> nent souvenir of an even more serious practice spill he
> suffered last year. The Jelineks are a fearless pair and
> in another sport they'd be called daredevils."

The passport to world fame was almost complete, but first they had to get to Prague. One of the American skaters, Dudley Richards who had placed second to Donald Jackson in the men's competition, suggested that the Jelineks and the rest of the Canadians in Philadelphia travel with the U.S. team to save time and hassle, but Otto was unable to cancel their reservations on the Canadian airline, and Sheldon Galbraith never even attempted to change the bookings for the rest of the team. "There's a lot of psychology in international skating. If we had flown with the American team, they would have received the lion's share of the publicity when we landed in Prague. We wanted to take care of our own public relations."

It was a smart decision, and one that ultimately saved the lives of the Canadian skaters. When they landed at Prague, they heard with shock that the plane carrying the American team had crashed at Brussels — killing all seventy-three people on board.

It was the worst disaster in skating history. In a few brief seconds, the team, and its accumulated years of experience, skill, and beauty, was completely wiped out. Gone were the new North American women's champion, Laurence Owen, her pairs' partner, Dudley Richards, her older sister, Mabel, and their mother, Mabel Vinson, who had competed against Canada's first world medal-winner, Cecil Smith, twenty years before. Gone too, were the friends and relatives who had unstintingly provided support and encouragement for their own skaters, and for hundreds of others.

Suddenly, a new gray cloud hung over the Jelinek's native city. The competition was immediately cancelled, and put forward to 1962, again in the Czech capitol.

Their second return to Prague was happier than the first. In spite of the air of repression, there was an underswell of resistance among the Czechs, often expressed openly. Wherever Otto and Maria went, there were crowds seeking autographs. Affectionate fans stopped them on the street, notes arrived at the hotel wishing them godspeed, and thousands of people turned out to watch them practice. They found time to visit their former home, now the

Austrian Embassy, and wander the streets Otto had once taken to school, and these emotional experiences strengthened their desire to win.

"The public knew we had been born in Prague and had escaped," said Otto. "Now we had come back behind the Iron Curtain to be one of them. We got showered with thousands of gifts, not only because we were top figure skaters, but because we were a symbol of freedom. As well as that, our biggest competitors in the pairs were the Russians."

For the first time in major competition the Jelineks had no family support at the rinkside. The guarantees of safety had not extended to their parents, who watched the championships from a hotel on the Jakobshorn high above Davos, where television reception was the best in Switzerland. Successful in a new life and surrounded by their Swiss friends, they thought back to the first time their children had performed at the Prague Winter Garden and now, fifteen years later, they waited for those children to skate on Czech ice once again.

The Prague stadium was packed with eighteen thousand devoted skating fans, cheering for the young expatriates. To music by the Czech composers Smetana and Dvořák, they were skating their best, blending artistic movements and long flowing edges with strong lifts and jumps, when, all at once, Maria landed badly and slid along the ice on one hand and knee.

At that moment, Mrs. Jelinek sat shredding paper napkins, her husband poured himself a whisky, spilling it over the edge of the glass, coach Bruce Hyland felt the bottom drop out of his stomach, and one hundred-and-fifty million television viewers wondered if this was the end for the Canadian pair. "Maria and Otto move back into their usual routine, still giving the impression of complete confidence," said ABC commentator Jim McKay. Another lift, a throw, and the audience was rapturous. "Brother and sister look almost exactly alike. They are almost exactly the same size. They are still skating as if they are held together by an elastic band, staying the same distance apart, moving in, moving out." Dick Button took over the commentary. "Watch Otto now. An Axel from a front spiral, and he catches Maria as she falls into a backward arch, which is the death spiral." The Dvořák melody swelled to a climax. "Now, two overhead lifts," Button continued, "done in opposite directions. Here comes the first overhead — the same now, again, but in the other direction — beautifully done." The audience agreed. At the finish, everyone was standing, shouting and applauding while Otto and Maria took their bows. Now they faced the agony of waiting, first for their marks, which were good, and then for the performance of the Russian pair, Ljudmila Belousova and Oleg Protopopov, which was flawless.

The tension was far greater than before the competition, and even their coach was convinced that the Russian team had edged them out. Then the results were announced. The Russians got three firsts from the judges, with ordinals totaling 16.5, but Otto and Maria got five first places, two seconds, and two thirds, giving them a total of 15 ordinals — and the gold medal.

It was a victory, not only for the Jelineks, but for the beleagured Czechs in the stands. As the Canadian couple skated their winning lap around the rink, people climbed right over the barriers onto the ice crying, "We won! We won!" Only they would know just how much that victory meant, but for the Jelineks, who went on to great success in the Ice Capades, it was the highlight of their career.

Donald Jackson, the first skater to perform a triple Lutz in international competition.

16

Good Guys Finish First

Donald Jackson, one of the finest figure skaters ever produced in Canada, started life as the kid on the block least likely to succeed in sport.

Born prematurely, he developed a double hernia as a baby and had to wear a truss for two years before undergoing surgery. He wasn't even able to walk until he was fifteen months old. Before he was four, he had contracted scarlet fever, a life-threatening disease in those days, and before he was eight, had developed pneumonia three times. His parents were warned that he would never be able to compete in sports like "normal" children, but even if this hadn't been the case, the idea of their gritty little boy taking up figure skating would have been the furthest thing from their minds. The Jacksons lived in the lower-income end of Oshawa — the industrial city where men were men and wore hockey skates to prove it. Any male with picks on the ends of his skates was considered to be the ultimate sissy and worthy of contemptuous jeers. As another skater remarked twenty years later, "Although many of us were exposed to the sport early in life, we came to regard it as an essentially effeminate activity — not quite as bad as violin lessons, but much less appealing than toboganning or heisting bubblegum from the corner store." Also, like violin lessons, it was an activity which called for a lot of training, which meant money — something the Jackson family didn't have very much of. As a result of all this, young Donald did not strap on a pair of skates until he was eight, and then he wore a pair of borrowed hockey skates so that he could compete in a fancy dress competition at his school winter carnival. He won the award for the best comic costume, his inability to stand upright on the ice undoubtedly contributing to his humorous appeal. Watching his schoolmates in the races, he became determined to learn how to skate so he could compete with them the following year.

A few weeks later, another window to the skating world was opened when he was taken to see an ice-show starring Barbara Ann Scott and Don Tobin. Now he didn't just want to learn to skate. He wanted to learn to skate like the men who had starred on the ice.

After a summer of pleading and reasoning, he was enrolled in the Oshawa Skating Club, where group lessons were conducted for the three hundred-and-fifty members. Unlike Barbara Ann Scott who had wanted "real" skates with picks, he revolted against the first pair his parents bought. They were white sissy skates meant for a girl, and he was simply not going to wear them. His father finally persuaded him to put them on after performing a hasty paint job.

The first lessons were in a large group, where the instructor, Alex Fulton, used games of tag to get all his young charges involved. Donald, smaller but faster than his peers, soon became a master of the fun games and his parents decided to splash out for one private lesson in figure skating each week under Nan Unsworth, at seventy-five cents for fifteen minutes. Soon Donald's enthusiasm for being on the ice spilled over onto the weekends, and his parents scoured the city for free school rinks where he could skate to his heart's content.

However, his career was almost ended before it ever really got under way. An attack of pneumonia put him in hospital, and within a few months his parents and his brother Bill followed him with lung infections. There was no hospital insurance then, and the crippling medical bills forced the Jacksons to use up their "rainy day" fund. A family conference was held to decide if they could afford to keep young Donald on skates, and if they could, whether or not to add two fifteen-minute free skating periods to his figure skating lesson. In the end they decided to budget the funds and let him try for one season. Soon after turning ten, he entered his first competition — the novice event at the Oshawa Skating Club. He was allowed to skate for two minutes exactly as he pleased. The effervescent Donald skated to the music of the Red Barn Polka, but as he attempted a straight forward two-footed spin, his feet got all tangled up and he ended up doing the infinitely more difficult cross-footed spin. Much to his surprise and the delight of the crowd, he won the event.

The same season he took the first of his basic tests, mandatory for those skaters who intend to skate competitively. Among the judges were Dick McLaughlin, president of the Ottawa club, and his wife Patsy, who were impressed with the free skating performance but failed him on his figures. Nevertheless, Nan Unsworth persuaded his parents that, not only did he have talent, but that he had the potential to become Canadian champion and they should consided sending him to a summer skating school at Cobourg, where she herself was one of the coaches. Donald's mother came along as well, as housekeeper for the summer; cooking, cleaning and scrubbing floors in return for the future champion's bed and board.

While the camp developed his free skating skills, it did little to progress his figures. Because he was small, he had problems making strong recognizable traces that would satisfy the judges, and he twice more failed his initial test.

In Oshawa, Ede Kiraly of Hungary, 1949 world pairs' champion and runner-up to Dick Button in the men's, had been hired by the skating club as head coach. He had been taught by one of Europe's top trainers, Arnold Gerschwiler of Switzerland, and under his direction, Donald quickly demonstrated his incredible ability to learn from watching when he landed a perfect Axel Paulsen on his first attempt. Unfortunately, he continued to fail his figures test until his seventh attempt when he finally passed out of sheer determination.

From the beginning, he produced spectacular jumps and the coach was convinced he had a pupil with more than Canadian championship potential. When he heard that Gerschwiler was going to be teaching at a summer school in Stratford, Ontario, he persuaded Donny's parents to open their purse strings one more time, and send the boy to study directly under the master.

Until then, Donald's life as a student had been relatively carefree. The big smile which split his face in two was the constant evidence of his enjoyment in skating, and his instructors had

138

always given him free rein to express his natural high spirits and sense of fun. Gerschwiler had a different outlook on life. Skating was a serious business, and this young lad that the Canadians thought so much of had better begin to realize it. He made him write out two hundred times, "I must not talk on patch," (the area where the skaters practiced figures), and forced him to relearn his double-loop jump which he had been doing off the right foot, so that he could do it off his left foot and use it in combination with others. He also helped his pupil master the double Salchow before sending him home again.

Under Wally Distelmyer, the new coach in Oshawa and former Canadian champion, Donald continued to build a solid competitive programme until 1952, when the family sadly realized the cost was becoming prohibitive and decided to pull him out. Kiraly, who was now running a summer school in Goderich, heard of the decision, and travelled to Oshawa to persuade the parents to reconsider. For the first time they heard someone they respected say that their son could become a world champion, but Kiraly went even further. He was so sure of his protégé's ability, that he said he would teach Donald himself without any charge for the lessons. The Jacksons gave in, and Donald continued to improve.

By age thirteen he was landing triple Salchows, but another potential block to his skating future came when the Oshawa club burned down. To gain ice time, members banded together and put on productions at other clubs and arenas, and Donald played a starring comedy role in "The Glad Rag Doll" using a life-size Raggedy Ann doll. On Sundays, Kiraly would come and take him to Peterborough for three hours of practice, and spend the rest of the day teaching his other pupils before ferrying Donald back home shortly before midnight. Then in March, 1954, two things happened — Arnold Gerschwiler invited Donny to England to train, and the renowned Minto Club in Ottawa asked him to skate in its carnival. There, for the first time, he was seen by the senior officials of both the club, and the Canadian Figure Skating Association. They were appalled that such a valuable skater might be lost to England, and resolved something had to be done to keep him in Canada. They decided to set up a sponsorship programme that would provide him with ice time at the Minto Club and accommodation in Ottawa during the winter. Otto Gold, whose rigid discipline had played such an important part in Barbara Ann Scott's success, was the top coach at the Minto Club, and when he agreed to train their son, the Jacksons knew there was no question of Donald going to England.

Before moving to Ottawa, he studied intensively at Gold's summer camp in Laval, Quebec, and passed his seventh test, becoming eligible for his first major competition, the Canadian Junior Championship, to be held in Toronto at the beginning of February, 1955.

While the championships were in progress, the more affluent members of the Minto Club stayed at the Royal York Hotel. The Jacksons stayed at the Ford Hotel which, before it was torn down, was to become the inn of last resort, and Donny was probably the most poorly equipped skater to try and win the crown. He had two pair of skates, one for figures and one for free skating, which cost $12.50 each, and only one pair of competition pants. Just before the free skating, he discovered he had left these precious pants back at the hotel, and stood around the dressing room, bare-legged and anxious, until his father fetched them to him with minutes to spare. Then he not only came first in the figures, a surprise to everybody except his coach, but performed so well in the free skating programme that he received one of the loudest and most prolonged ovations ever heard at Varsity Arena. With the title came recognition from many sources, including the city of Oshawa. Requests poured in from all over Ontario for performances at shows and carnivals, and an Oshawa family, the Dillinghams, offered to make up any expenses the family couldn't meet.

With the major financial burden eased, Donald was able to spend the summer in Lake Placid with Otto Gold working on the figures necessary to pass his eighth and final test and be eligible for his first senior championships at Galt in 1956, where he skated strongly against defending champion Charles Snelling, placing second.

The following year, he competed in the North American Championships where he fell four times and placed, coincidentally, fourth, and the Canadian Championships where he placed second. At the World Championships in Colorado Springs, his figures pulled a fifth-place free skating performance down, but he still ended up seventh in the world.

While he was at the World's, young Jackson learned some of

the rules of gamesmanship and first developed a relationship with Sheldon Galbraith that was to pay long term dividends. While practicing his jumps in preparation for the competition, he met his old part-time coach Arnold Gerschwiler who was travelling with an English skater, Michael Brooker. Gerschwiler commented on the improvement in Donald's jumps and asked him to do some more, and more, and more. The young skater was pleased at the interest his former trainer was showing. Another spectator was not. Sheldon Galbraith, Canadian team coach, approached the couple and suggested that Jackson had done enough for one day and needed to rest up for the competition. The wiley Gerschwiler thanked Jackson, nodded and left. A few more minutes of overtraining could have taken the edge off the Canadian's performance.

Back in Ottawa, problems developed in his relationship with his coach. Gold's daughter Frances, now on the edge of competitive skating, was taking up larger amounts of her father's teaching time, and sixteen-year-old Donald was being asked on a daily basis to demonstrate new moves and techniques for her benefit. He was advised to change coaches, and after much deliberation decided on Pierre Brunet, who taught in New York and coached a group of world class skaters including reigning world champion, Carol Heiss. So Donald moved to a flea-bag hotel in New York to study at the New York Skating Club. Unfortunately, this ended the sponsorship from Ottawa, and the family was thrown back on the joint earnings of George Jackson, $60 a week, and Pat, $45.

In the next two years, under Brunet's guidance, he moved steadily up the ladder, winning both the Canadian title and the North American. Then at the World's, again at Colorado Springs, he signalled that he was moving into place for a serious run at the number one spot when he won the silver medal, coming second to the American skater, David Jenkins, who captured his third world title in a row, and established an incredible family record. David and his brother, Hayes Alan, had held the world title for seven successive years between them.

Jackson's marks were impressive, and the judges left no doubts about who they believed was the rightful heir to the throne. All seven awarded him second place in the free skating, in which his performance was described as sensational. He opened his solo with a double Lutz jump and produced Axel Paulsens first from one foot, then the other. "His triple Salchow and delayed double Salchow were beautiful and breathtaking. Jackson has the ability to jump into the air as if he were catapulted by a steel spring."

In January 1961, he passed another milestone in his career. He captured his third Canadian title in Montreal, and achieved his first perfect mark after the free skating performance, during which he performed two jumps never before attempted by a skater in national competition — a split double Lutz and a cross-over Axel. A few weeks later in Philadelphia, he won the North American title for the second time, ahead of Bradley Lord, the U.S. champion, skating with a temperature of 103°, then returned to New York for his final training spell with Brunet before flying to the World Championships in Prague. Because he could not afford the extra air fare to fly home and go to the competition from there, his parents informed the C.F.S.A. that he would fly with the American team from New York, but his high temperature continued to plague him. Finally the doctor ordered him to bed and told him he would have to catch a later plane. Shortly afterwards, the terrible plane crash occurred over Brussels, killing the entire American team including Donald's recent opponent, Bradley Lord.

Lying in bed gave him time to think about this tragedy and the odd way he had escaped it, and to reflect on other things as well — his life, his career, and finally, his skating coach. Most of the young skaters who had been in Brunet's school had dispersed or retired and there was little incentive for Donald to stay in New York when the element of competition seemed to have gone. He decided he wanted to be coached by the man who had always shown him such fairness and understanding — Sheldon Galbraith. So in the summer of 1961, he made the journey up to Schumacher where so many Canadian and world stars had been to train with the former U.S. Navy pilot instructor.

Galbraith, the perfectionist, philosopher and father figure, knew that Jackson was star quality, but had to lay down the ground rules for the latest addition to his roster of champions and show who was boss. He made the young skater take off on a jump and cross his legs exactly opposite to the way he was used to. As he soared above the ice, Donald realized he was going to have a fall and knew it was going to be a bad one. "I came down heavily on one thigh, and it really hurt. Mr Galbraith walked across and said, 'Fine! I saw exactly what I wanted to see. Now let's get on with the skating.' I never did know what it was he was looking for.''

It was the beginning of a relationship that was to blast Jackson from perfectly acceptable world class jumping and spinning into the kind of explosive skating which would not be equaled for many years after his retirement from competition. ''I was three-quarters of the way up the ladder when Galbraith first took me on. He analyzed everything I did, and in his efforts to find a better way of doing something he would sometimes make me take steps back down, but when he was finished, I had ended up at the top.''

During that summer, Donald also managed to land one of the most difficult jumps in skating — the triple Lutz. To do this, he had to get speed going backwards, dig in with the one toe and take off on a back outside edge, doing three complete revolutions in the air, and then come down on the back outside edge of the toe-assisting foot. It was a jump which had never been done successfully in competition, and although Donald continued to practice it throughout the fall and winter, he only managed to land four more good ones out of five hundred.

As the 1962 World Championships in Prague approached, Donald and Galbraith concentrated all their attention on the five-minute free skating programme, paying special need to the intricate footwork between the more spectacular jumps. Jackson arrived several days before the event and worked daily on his routine, and on Sunday, March 11, he had his first practice at the arena in the Fucik Sports Hall, where ten thousand spectators were on hand to watch the free skating workouts.

The competition started with the school figures, and Donald was doing quite well, keeping a close second to the home-town favorite, Karol Divin, until the fourth figure, when he laid his circles out of line on clean ice and then tried to correct his error. Although his fifth and sixth figures were excellent, he still ended up a whopping forty-five points behind the leader. The enormous task he now faced was to make up this deficit in the free skating, and convince at least five of the judges to give him first place.

It was time to consider putting the almost impossible triple Lutz into the programme after all. Galbraith wasn't sure that it was absolutely necessary, particularly when he considered the enormous odds against success. Donald, however, was adamant about wanting to try it, at least.

Safety or chance.

Ultimately it would be his choice, but until the very moment of truth, the decision to do the triple Lutz remained up in the air.

OUR GUEST OF HONOUR

Donald Jackson

WORLD CHAMPION — MEN'S FIGURE SKATING
PRAGUE, CZECHOSLOVAKIA, MARCH 15th, 1962

ON THE OCCASION OF A TESTIMONIAL DINNER BY THE CITY OF OSHAWA
AT HOTEL GENOSHA ON TUESDAY, APRIL 3rd, 1962

Programme for reception in Oshawa honouring Donald Jackson's World Championship victory in 1962.

17

Room at the Top

The warm-up was like hundreds Donny had done before — a leisurely tour of the rink to study the condition of the surface and identify any high and low spots, a build-up in speed to get the blood flowing and the muscles relaxed, and a quick practice run through the intended jumps, including a modest triple Lutz with a two-footed landing. Less than half-an-hour before, Karol Divin had skated an excellent free programme and received a series of 5.7s from the judges. He was firmly out in front, although Jackson didn't know the actual marks, and it looked as if the only battle left was for second place and the silver medal. Certainly there was nothing in Donald's warm-up to alert the crowd or the judges there was anything other than a competent performance to come — nothing except the ever-widening grin on the face of the kid from Oshawa. The warm-up completed, he looked up at Galbraith in the stands, and gave him the thumbs-up signal. He was ready to do the triple Lutz.

Just before performing, he stood at ice edge with his coach: the difficult jump uppermost in their minds. "Do you think I can do it?" Jackson asked. "Don," Galbraith replied. "There is always room at the top." With a smile, Donald skated out onto the ice, and into the history books.

Dick Button, five times world champion, was commentating for ABC-TV with sportscaster, Jim McKay. Button had watched Jackson in practice, and had sensed that something unique might take place that night. McKay was more cautious in opening the commentary of what was to become one of the most widely repeated television sports broadcasts ever made. "This is Donald Jackson of Canada. He is 21 years old. If he is going to win the World Championship tonight . . . he must give the greatest performance of his life." Jackson spread his arms, and launched into what Button called, "one of the finest 'come-from-behind' skating performances ever seen," done to the music from Bizet's Carmen. There was no dramatic build-up to the triple Lutz — just some lightening-fast footwork.

Then, right knee bent, Donald shoved his toe firmly into the ice and pushed off — legs eighteen inches apart. As he sprang into the air, his feet came together, his arms folded across his chest, and he began to spin — one, two, three times, almost faster than the eye could follow — then landed perfectly, his arms spread wide, his smile radiant.

Millions of television viewers heard Dick Button shout, "A beautiful triple Lutz! It's fantastic!" then the loudest crowd roar in the history of skating welled up in the stadium and drowned out the music. Jackson did two complete turns, a series of half-turns and some incredible footwork before he could even hear the music again, and then, the tension of the Lutz over, he skated as ever — for the enjoyment of the sport. Jumps and turns that alone would have made a championship performance, followed each other in rapid succession; a double flip jump, two walley jumps, a perfect double Salchow.

McKay excitedly informed the television audience, "If Jackson can give one of the great performances of all time, he can win. Otherwise, he cannot . . . Looking at our unofficial figures here, it looks as if Jackson would have to have marks of either 5.9 or 6.0, which is perfection, from almost every judge in order to have even a chance of catching Divin. It's almost impossible." Another turn, and into the air for two-and-a-half revolutions, a landing on the left foot, and another yell of approval for the double Axel, a three-turn, and one more double Axel. A pause, a change in tempo, more intricate footwork, turns, a second double flip, a sliding stop in time with the music. He was halfway through his five-minute programme. Two single Axels in opposite directions, another stop and then the hand-clapping beat of the Habanera passage, Jackson skating in perfect time to the music, a delayed double Salchow, a one-foot Axel leading into a flying camel spin, a spectacular triple Salchow, a flying sit-spin, landed cleanly and converted into an upright spin. The crowd yelled, stamped and clapped its approval. A double loop, a double toe-loop, a final double Lutz and a double Lutz and Axel combination, and his final sit-spin once more leading to an upright spin, and it was over.

He bowed to the spectators, every one of them on their feet delivering a massive ovation, then the first set of marks went up from the nine judges. For artistic impression, seven awarded him 5.9, one 5.8, and one 6.0. Then the marks for technical merit, a 5.8, two 5.9s, and six 6.0s, for a total of seven perfect marks, a record not equaled by any singles competitor since.

Karol Divin told him in the dressing room, "The competition is very close. I would like to tell you that if I win, I wish to give my gold medal to you — you were the greatest in this competition."

As it happened, Divin's gesture was made unnecessary, for when the dust cleared Donald Jackson had won the gold medal. He had been placed first by all nine judges in the free skating, and in the combined voting, he had received five first places and four seconds. Canada had its first men's world champion.

"I don't think I really appreciated what had happened until I got back home. When I stepped onto the podium I was proud to represent my country, and proud of having done well, but the main thing was — I had skated my best."

Galbraith, who certainly deserved to share in the victory, was ecstatic for his pupil. "It was a thrilling experience. I cried. I couldn't remember ever having seen a performance that was up to that level, such a tremendous one-man show." Dick Button summed up the feelings of skaters, commentators, and millions of fans. "This was a moment that will stand as one of the greatest in skating history."

After the championships, Jackson went on a world tour, then returned home to Oshawa where fifteen thousand fellow citizens turned out to greet him. The mayor of "General Motors City" appropriately presented him with a new car, which he declined so he could remain an amateur and compete in the 1964 Olympics. Galbraith was convinced that by then, Jackson would have completed at least a quadruple Lutz, and other firsts in competition.

But in the end, Donald decided that he could no longer afford to remain amateur. All his skating life, his parents had done without to get him to this peak. Now he could stop the scrimping with the endless pileup of debts, and begin to repay them. He joined the Ice Follies, and skated four hundred-and-twenty shows a year for seven years.

In the Ice Follies he met and married Joanne Diercks, and eventually left the show to raise their five children and run the Donald Jackson Skate Company. But still, over twenty years after his world record performance, he loves to skate in professional championships, shows, and charity events, and happily gives his time to open a rink in honor of Barbara Ann Scott, or perform in the annual Bursary Skating show to raise money for other young skaters.

Donald Jackson, champion, has never forgotten what others did to help him reach the top.

Donald McPherson and Wendy Griner returning from the 1963 World Championships.

18

A Forgotten Hero

"Timing is so important," said pairs champion, Robert Paul.

Often, the light of accomplishment shines pale when it comes too close to the brightness of some more powerful star. Canadian skating champion, Donald McPherson, performing in the circle of brilliance surrounding Donald Jackson, flashed so briefly in the skating sky that no one seems to have recorded his stellar presence.

Although he was Canadian junior champion at fourteen in 1959, and the youngest skater ever to win the world's men's event in 1963, his accomplishments went largely unnoticed. The Canadian Press files show no photographs whatsoever of McPherson, although some lesser skaters have nice fat files all to themselves, and those of the Toronto Star, the paper with Canada's largest circulation including Windsor, where McPherson was born, and Stratford, where he trained, were almost equally bereft of pictures. There was only one photograph — showing McPherson returning from his gold medal performance at the World Championships along with Wendy Griner, who had placed fourth in the ladies' competition. The picture was in Miss Griner's file.

An attempt to find film footage of McPherson, for a television special on the Canadian skaters who had won gold medals in world competition, met with a similar astonishing lack of success. The only film in existence seemed to be some home-movie footage of the young skater performing his figures at the 1963 Cortina World Championships, taken by Sheldon Galbraith. The irony is that for Donald McPherson, skating was, and has remained to this day, his whole life.

Like Donald Jackson he came from a family of slender means, but unlike the Oshawa youngster, the decision for him to skate came from his family. "I started skating when I was two years old. We lived in a very small apartment in the middle of town, and there was no place for me to go out and play. My mother read in a newspaper that a skating club was starting in the fall, so she got me a pair of skates." And off he went. His desire to excel grew quickly, and by the time he was six he was already entering and winning small competitions.

The daily routine, like those of other competitors, revolved around skating and school. "As a skater you more or less have to give up any sort of private life, because there is only time for study and practice, but if you really love it, as I did and as I do, then really you are giving up nothing. My skating helped me tremendously at school because I was forced to concentrate, and would finish my homework earlier so that I could do more skating."

His first international appearance was at the 1960 Squaw Valley Olympics, where as a fifteen-year-old, he gained an insight into the stresses of top level competition. He placed eighth at the World's in Vancouver the same year, then in 1961 won the silver medal in the Canadian Championships behind Donald Jackson, and placed fifth in the North American Championships his first time out. With the World Championships in Prague cancelled, he had to wait until 1962 to demonstrate his improvement under coach Dennis Silverthorne, and this he did ably.

Somewhat eclipsed by Jackson's astonishing come-from-behind performance, seventeen-year-old McPherson's free skating programme nevertheless received second-best marks. Five of the nine judges placed him second, three placed him third, and only the French judge awarded him a fourth place ordinal. Again, he was let down by his figures which counted for sixty percent of the points.

With Jackson's decision to turn professional, the other Donald had a chance to shine alone and maintain the continuity of the Canadian golds, but lack of money was a constant problem. He captured the 1963 Canadian and North American titles, but to get to the World Championships in Cortina, Italy, in March, his father had to cash in an insurance policy.

The topsy-turvey marking at the competition gave him

placements in his figures which ranged from second to as low as sixth, but this time he dominated the free skating, receiving eight firsts and one second.

Alain Calmat of France, the reigning bronze medalist, had equally unequal votes for his figures, ranging from first place from the U.S. judge, to sixth from the Canadian, J.A. McKechnie.

In the final analysis, and under the quaint judging system of skating, McPherson, with five second-place votes overall, became the winner and the youngest man ever to win the gold at a World Championship.

Getting there was more than half the fun for McPherson. "To be a champion, you have to have the desire to prove that you can be the best, even if it means giving up everything else. It's a marvelous feeling when you finally achieve your goal, but the work along the way means so much more."

Nineteen sixty-four was an Olympic year, and the new world champion had to decide whether he could afford to stay an amateur long enough to try for the gold at Innsbruck. Unfortunately, the problem was solved for him by a complete lack of funds, so that when he received a good offer from the European skating show, Holiday on Ice, he turned professional.

When he decided to remain and live in Europe, his total invisibility in Canada and the Canadian media was assured. Once, while battling diabetes, he fell and received a serious head injury. This caused an aneurysm and McPherson was locked into a personal battle for over a year trying to bring himself up to a peak level of fitness. He succeeded and got back into the show, but never, in all that time, did one line of copy appear in his homeland.

He never regretted his decision to move to Europe. Twenty-one years after winning his world title he said, "It has been an advantage to me. I've had the opportunity to work with people like John Curry, Toller Cranston, Robin Cousins and other great skaters. It's been a wonderful experience."

But Donald McPherson, the last gleam of gold before Canada entered the decade-long dark age of men's skating, still remains the forgotten man in his own country.

Dutch-born Petra Burka, Canada's 1965 World Champion.

19

A Power Play

The skating jump called the Salchow was originated by the great Ulrich Salchow during the Edwardian era, and eventually developed into the triple Salchow, where the skater takes off from a back inside edge, does three revolutions in the air, then comes down on the back outside edge of the opposite foot. No woman skater had ever landed the jump in competition until fifteen-year-old Petra Burka included it in her programme at the Canadian Senior Women's Championship at Toronto's Varsity Arena in 1962.

Although it all happened so fast that few of the five thousand spectators realized what she had achieved, members of the skating world, including Donald Jackson and former national champion and coach Osborne Colson, were very impressed and agreed that not only had she done it, but done it beautifully.

Her mother's reaction, that it wasn't too important and that Petra did the double Axel much better, was a little more cautious in light of the fact that her mother, Ellen Burka, Dutch figure skating champion of 1946, was also her coach. She knew better than most the all-round ability of her young and talented pupil, and was impressed enough to be objective.

Petra's life as a skater had started nine years earlier. At the age of six, she was given her first pair of skates and taken to an open air rink in North Toronto, where she ended up skating as if she had been doing it for years. When she was ten her mother saw her potential and started training her in earnest, and although she would only grow to a little over five feet and one inch, she was built strongly enough to execute the difficult jumps and turns normally thought to be the prerogative of male skaters. Having a mother for a coach had its advantages and disadvantages, but at thirteen Petra definitely decided she had to get away. Mrs. Burka sent her to Rochester, to study under Donald Laws who would later coach Scottie Hamilton.

Back in Toronto in 1961, she won the Canadian junior title. Within a year she had performed her record-making triple Salchow, and competed in the World's at Prague placing fourth — with one judge giving her a first place mark in free skating, and three considering her worth second place. It was an impressive performance, and the door was open to international recognition and honors.

In 1963, she fell back one place in the world standing, and realized that the international judges were looking for more than spectacular jumps — they wanted to see graceful movements. So she started to take ballet lessons, and to concentrate harder on her figures. "I had found figures boring, and then, when I actually began to enjoy doing them, my performance got better."

It improved to the point where, in 1964, she deposed Wendy Griner as Canadian champion. Then, at the Innsbruck Olympics she skated what the Toronto Star described as "a dazzling performance," unfortunately overshadowed by the outstanding performance of Sjoukje Dijkstra, who skated an incredible programme and received six 5.9s for technical merit from the nine judges. Petra placed third.

Her upward rise in skating wasn't reflected in her social life however. "I didn't have time to go to school at regular hours, as my life revolved around the ice rink. I only went to school the first and last terms, but still managed to get good marks because of the discipline skating put into my life. I missed out on a lot of parties and was never asked out on a date. I thought I would never meet anyone. I think boys were afraid of me. In Grade 12 at Lawrence Park Collegiate, I had to make a speech about my travels and accomplishments as a skater, so they put me on a pedestal instead of considering me their equal."

In 1965 she won the triple crown of Canadian skating; the Canadian Championship, the North American Championship, and the World Championship. At the World's in Colorado Springs, she was placed first by all nine judges. Behind her were Regine Heitzer of Austria and Peggy Fleming of the United States. Back in Canada she was voted top female athlete for the second year in a row, and the road looked clear for a long successful journey, and perhaps an Olympic gold in 1968.

The next year she was all set to defend her world title in Davos, but first she had to win the Canadian Championship at Peterborough which most people considered, under the circumstances, to be a mere formality. Surely the best female skater in the world would also be the best in Canada. Apparently not.

One of the judges, Dr. Suzanne Francis, awarded a higher score in the free skating to an unknown thirteen-year-old from Vancouver, Karen Magnussen. "This was tantamount to Canada's national hockey team losing to the Toronto Marlboro Juniors in their last game before leaving for the world championships," said Gordon Lethbridge, Canadian dance champion, and a competitor at the 1966 World's.

At first the Americans were astounded by this Canadian turncoat of events, then quick to take advantage of it to boost the chances of their own champion — Peggy Fleming. By the time Petra reached Davos, word had spread that she had lost her touch and couldn't even match a teenager from her own country.

Bowing to pressure to look svelte on the ice, she had gone on a strict diet and lost twenty-five pounds. Instead of being praised for her accomplishment, the judges started to maintain that she would obviously have lost her strength in the free skating and in the figures. Apparently she would now be too light to cut deep figures into the hard outdoor ice at Davos. Her own country hadn't been behind her one hundred percent, so now the rest of the world was out to get her.

"We sensed the feeling in Europe as soon as we arrived," said Lethbridge. "We on the team should have gotten together and fought. We should have protected Petra."

The pressures were too much. Petra lost her confidence and her competitive edge, and after trailing Peggy Fleming in the figures, wanted to withdraw. Her mother persuaded her to continue, but it was no good — more disasters followed, and she missed badly on two of her toughest jumps. As a result, she lost her title and was placed third.

A few weeks later, Petra signed a professional contract with

Holiday on Ice, and spent three years touring Europe and North America. Eighteen years afterward she remembered, "At that time there were a lot of expectations for me to win again. I probably didn't skate as well as I could have, but I think I learned a lot more from losing than I ever did from winning. It was a rude awakening but extremely enlightening. Now I see that losing is not such a major crime. I won a world championship and I will always carry that with me, but being third in the world is nothing to be ashamed of. As a professional skater, I was plunked down into another crazy environment. The first year I travelled through almost every country in Eastern and Western Europe. It was a lot of work — fourteen shows a week. I consider it in some ways an incredible education. I learned languages, visited museums. I was still only nineteen, and the pro world opened my eyes a lot. The people I dealt with in the show were like gypsies, many of them had been around for years, and they liked to party. I trained every day and went to bed early to read books, to learn about history and study languages."

In the end Petra decided to come back to Canada and set down roots.

Nowadays, she still lives by the philosophy which made her a good champion and a contented professional — don't be afraid of making mistakes, know your limitations, and be happy in yourself.

Karen Magnussen won the British Columbia Coast Champion-ship at age 10, and later went on to become World Champion.

20

A Political Scene

Five years followed Petra Burka's last medal-winning performance before a skater would establish Canada, once again, in the international record books. During this time, many hopes rested with the young Karen Magnussen, who although only thirteen when she astonished the skating community with a dazzling free skating programme in the 1966 Canadian Championships, was proving to be a gutsy skater with nerves of steel in the competitive arena.

Skating began for six-year-old Karen, and her friend and future opponent Cathy Lee Irwin, with a five dollar pair of skates on a public rink in Vancouver. As the two little blonde girls tripped and slid around the ice, their watching mothers decided that they should enroll them in the Kerrisdale Skating Club, beginning skating careers that would produce two Canadian junior champions, and for Karen, three world gold medals. With her all the way was her mother Gloria, smoothing paths, arranging finances, giving encouragement and support. "As you are working your way up the ladder there are a lot of different things that go wrong. Those things were buffered by my mother, but she was never a pushy 'skating mother.'"

Karen's first coach, Dr. Helmut May, had impressive credentials. In addition to his Doctorate in economics, he had competed for Austria in the 1936 Winter Olympics at Garmisch-Partenkirchen, Germany, and in the World's in Paris, and in two succeeding Olympics. While he taught Karen on the ice, his wife Doris, a graduate of the Vienna Academy of Dance, taught her ballet dancing, which she continued throughout her amateur skating life. Within a year she had passed her preliminary figure test and started a steady forward progress that she maintained for the next ten years.

When the North Shore Winter Club opened in 1960, it filled a large skating gap in the city that had built Canada's first indoor rink. It was nearer to the Magnussen's home on Thorncliffe Drive, and Karen was among the first to join. With the change in location came a change of coaches, this time to Edi Rada, who was such a strong disciplinarian that he lost many young skaters who could not stand the pace. Rada, born in Vienna, had the unique record of having been the national champion of Germany, Switzerland, Poland and Austria, at a time when national championships in Europe were open events.

Nicknamed "Gestapo" by some of his students, he imposed exercise punishments for late arrival. While some parents and children accepted his authoritarian approach, others resented it, and there were occasional clashes with Mrs. Magnussen when he followed the Otto Gold routine of never praising a pupil. But the taskmaster got results. One year the five girls competing for the British Columbia Sectional Championships were all his pupils.

Under his guidance Karen amassed competitive skating experience, medals, and trophies, but in 1964, when Rada was vacationing in Austria, Mrs. Magnussen asked the other Winter Club pro, Linda Brauckmann, to take over the teaching duties. The new relationship was to continue until Karen left amateur performance. Mrs. Brauckmann, who had received her instruction from Otto Gold, was another link in the chain of Canadian skating success. She and Mrs. Magnussen were both at the Canadian Junior Championships in Calgary in 1965 when Karen made her first move into the skating spotlight by coming first. She made a bad start in the figures, placing twentieth and thirteenth in the first two, and she and her coach had their only major confrontation when Mrs. Brauckmann tore into the unhappy skater. Karen later complained to her mother but she supported the coach, and in the next three figures, Karen went out and won two, and placed second in the other, placing fifth overall. Her free skating then took her to the title.

The following year, at the Canadian Championships, she came in fourth, after receiving a mark of 5.9 for artistic impression from Dr. Suzanne Francis, the mark that worked against Petra Burka. In the free skating, Karen was placed second, and Ed Waring of the Globe and Mail said, "she stole the hearts of the fans and most of the judges."

At the same championships, Dr. Charles Snelling regained his place on Canada's world team. Snelling, who reigned as Canadian Champion during Donald Jackson's emerging years, was the iron man of Canadian skating. He became Canadian junior champion in 1952, and won the first of five successive senior titles in 1954. He took the bronze medal at the 1957 World Championships in Colorado Springs, but by 1958, he had decided on a career in medicine and found it too difficult to combine the demands of medical school and competition training. He won the Canadian title for the last time in 1958. Donald Jackson, who became a lifelong friend, and Eddie Collins, were rocking the throne and according to Snelling, "The title could have gone to any one of us three. They both beat me at the World's in Paris three weeks later."

Throughout his university years, he skated in carnivals and as part of a comedy act with a friend, but when his schooling ended he returned to the competitve field, winning the men's title in 1964. He placed second in '65 and '66, then retired again to continue his interest in the sport as a judge. He had one of the longest skating careers in the country, spanning seventeen years from 1950 to 1967.

It was in 1967, Snelling's retirement year, that Karen Magnussen increased her standing by coming second in the national competition, and qualified for the Canadian team which would compete in the North American and World Championships. In the North American's, held in Montreal, she was placed fourth behind world champion Peggy Fleming whose programme had been choreographed by former Olympic champion, Robert Paul. At Karen's international debut at the World's in Vienna, she came twelfth.

The next year the Canadian Championships took place at the Kerrisdale rink, Karen's first skating home. She took a clear lead in the compulsory figures, and then brought the crowd to its feet with a stunning free skating performance. Her points totalled 1823.3, and a first place vote from all seven judges, gave Canada its first woman champion from out west.

Behind her was Linda Carbonetto of Toronto, with 1,718.7 points. For the home crowd it was one of the greatest weeks in skating history as B.C. captured all four titles. Jay Humphrey won the men's, Betty and John McKilligan the pairs, and Joni Graham and Don Phillips, the dance.

Karen was now set for her first crack at Olympic honors and was to witness in Grenoble, and later in 1968 at the World's in Geneva, the last amateur performances of Peggy Fleming, the graceful, dark-haired American champion whose fragile appearance belied her stamina. Grenoble attracted 1,293 competitors, with 228 women — a number which almost matched the total entry of the 1924 Olympics, when Cecil Smith competed at Chamonix. Sixty thousand people packed into a specially constructed amphitheater to witness President de Gaulle declare the games open, and for the first time a figure skater, former world champion Alain Calmat, brought in the Olympic torch. Thousands of artificial roses were dropped from helicopters, the five Olympic rings were etched in colored smoke against the blue sky, and the Olympic flags fluttered down on parachutes. The games had come a long way in forty-four years.

Peggy Fleming won the Olympic gold, receiving marks of 5.9 out of a perfect 6.0 from every one of the judges for her free skating.

Karen, eighth after the figures, had skated to a fourth place in the free skating and ended up seventh overall. Her free skating, however, captured the attention of observers from every country. Carlo Fassi, Peggy Fleming's coach, predicted that Karen could win, "should win," the 1972 Olympics. The Christian Science Monitor correspondent, Monty Hoyt, a former American champion, said that Karen's performance eclipsed the defending champions "with an electrifying programme that put her name on every tongue."

The World Championships were a virtual replay of the Olympics — once again Peggy Fleming took the title and Karen was placed seventh — but already the Canadian girl's reputation as a free skater was established, and on her return to Vancouver, invitations for skating performances came from all over the world.

In 1968, the Canadian Championships returned to Toronto, and sadly for Karen Magnussen, so did the women's title with the brilliant performance of Linda Carbonetto. This vivacious nineteen-year-old pupil of Ellen Burka's had had her training interrupted by illness or injury for three successive years, but in 1969 she completed a full season, and her good looks, sparkle, and on-ice showmanship led to continual offers from professional companies. Finally, after the World Championships in Oakland, California later in the year, she left the amateur competitions behind forever when she signed with a major ice show. Before the Canadian Championships, however, she was being rapturously touted as a bringer-home of gold.

"There isn't a competitive skater in the world who's received the sort of offers with which she has been bombarded by every ice show in the business," wrote Jim Proudfoot of the Toronto Star, who described her as "the brightest ornament" of Canadian skating, and "perhaps this nation's next great international champion."

Linda, outclassed in the figures the previous year when she trailed Karen by eighty-four points, finished the 1969 compulsories almost level with the defending champion. The '68-'69 season was also the year that for the first time, marks for figures counted fifty instead of sixty percent of the total. Coaches like Sheldon Galbraith and Mrs. Ellen Burka wanted even further reductions, and were backed by most competitive skaters. "The rules for school figures were made before the theory of flight was established and they are out of date," said Galbraith. He wanted the compulsory figures cut to forty percent and the competitor given the option of doing figures of his choice for the other ten percent, a similar system to the "world" competitions in which Louis Rubenstein competed in 1890.

Karen made several mistakes in her free skating programme and fell once. As defending champion she was awarded good scores, but an opening was left for Linda if she skated flawlessly, which she did. "Miss Carbonetto, of course, realized that she could win last night only if she was superb," wrote Proudfoot. "She was better than that: she was perfect. One judge even gave her performance that rating, six out of six."

But, impressed as the judges were with Linda's performance, the potential of Karen was not overlooked. "It would be a grave error to dismiss Karen Magnussen, who's only sixteen," said Proudfoot. "Despite her errors last night, she still got first place from three of the judges.''

Both skaters were invited to compete in the World's at Colorado Springs. The third place singles skater and Karen's longtime companion, Cathy Lee Irwin, and a rising young star from Lachine, Quebec, Toller Cranston, were added to the team for the North American Championships in Oakland, California.

This event was held every two years, alternating between Canada and the United States. Winning was assumed to guarantee a favorable reception at the World's, where prejudging was not uncommon. The host country provided four out of the seven judges, and this time it was America's turn. Karen won the compulsories, and in the free skating many people, including Karen herself, thought she had given one of her best performances ever, but still the title went to the American Champion, Janet Lynn, who was 1.4 points ahead.

The next day, the U.S. judges seemed to be tumbling all over themselves to cover up their tracks, and awarded the ice dancing title to Canadian champions Donna Taylor and Bruce Lennie, ranked twelfth in the world, over their own pair Judy Schwomeyer and Jim Sladky, ranked third. Jim Proudfoot wrote ''The judging was so laughably inconsistent that Canadian officials admitted they'd begun to question the value of participation in any form.'' There was a terrific uproar from all sides signalling the demise of the North American Championships which were to be held only once more.

In spite of the debacle, however, the competition served to enforce the race toward the gold between Janet Lynn and Karen Magnussen. Everyone wondered which of the two young skaters would be placed higher in the upcoming World's in Colorado Springs. The question proved to be academic as Karen was unable to compete. She had gone to Squaw Valley between championships, and although she had been warned that the pains in her legs could be shin splints, she continued to train. The day before the competition she became almost crippled from stress fractures and was banned from skating. She watched the championships from a wheelchair.

Janet Lynn placed fifth, and right behind her was Linda Carbonetto one place higher than Karen had achieved the previous year. Once again, the judging was severely criticized and subject to catcalls from the crowd, as it seemed to be based on previous performances of the various skaters rather than what had recently taken place on the ice. Jim Proudfoot wrote, "It damages skating when judges are staring off into space instead of watching the athletes, suggesting they've made up their minds in advance. And the marks they post often reinforce that suspicion."

Thirty-six days later, shortly before her seventeenth birthday, Karen was back on skates, preparing to recapture her Canadian title at Edmonton in 1970. The only other serious contender, since Linda Carbonetto had turned professional, was Cathy Lee Irwin, now skating out of the Toronto Cricket Skating and Curling Club. At the end of the compulsory figures, Karen led the field by 20.9 points, and after the free skating, all seven judges voted to put her back on the throne she had been forced to vacate for a year.

By now, Karen had graduated from high school and enrolled in the new Simon Fraser University. Here, along with other athletes, she became a guinea pig for a series of kinesiology studies at the University of British Columbia — studies which indicated that four minutes of hard skating equaled one hour of basketball. In addition to her skating and regular classes, she studied ballet five times a week under Madame Lydia Karpova, a graduate of the St. Petersburg Imperial School, filling a timetable that would daunt all but the strongest wills. "A lot of people underestimate me, how gutsy I am," she told one journalist.

At the 1970 World Championships in Ljubljana, Yugoslavia, Karen was placed fourth behind defending champion Gaby Seyfert of East Germany, while Janet Lynn fell back one place to sixth, then took her third Canadian title at Winnipeg in 1971 with one of her better figures performances and received 5.9 from six of seven judges for artistic impression in the free skate.

Two weeks later she skated a personal best in figures and an outstanding free skating performance which earned her a perfect six from one judge and the support of two of the three U.S. judges to give her the North American title over Janet Lynn. With East Germany's Gabriele Seyfert retired, skating authorities in the United States had been gleefully predicting Janet Lynn as the logical successor to the world crown. Now Canadian sports writers decided it was their turn and, just as gleefully, took to forecasting a new Canadian world champion at the 1971 World Championships in Lyon, France. "The threat from Europe seems minimal now. The new champion there is Beatrix Schuba of Austria, a girl who simply isn't in the same class as the two who competed here," wrote one authority, foolishly and summarily dismissing the up-and-coming young skater who had trained in the summer with Sheldon Galbraith.

To the surprise of no one except the various sports writers in North American cities, Trixi Schuba came first, winning her first world title. Julie Holmes of the United States took the silver medal, and Karen stepped onto the international podium for the first time when she won the bronze. It was while these young girls were in the process of receiving their awards that the producers at ABC television twisted the facts to suit their own purposes, and perpetrated a fraud on the American viewers. As the crowd applauded for the three medalists, the television cameras focused on another unauthorized podium where Janet Lynn, who had finished fourth, was standing. The announcer explained that Janet had completely won the hearts of the French audience, and that all the applause was for her. Trixi, in what should have been the moment of her greatest triumph after years of hard and heart-breaking work, had to be consoled instead by the two other winners. It was a blatant example of the media moulding an event to suit the image which suited it best, and a great many people were extremely upset by the incident, including the U.S. team manager Charles DeMore, who later apologized for the whole thing although he had nothing to do with it.

The 1972 Canadian Championships at London, Ontario, acted as a curtain raiser to the Olympics in Sapporo, Japan and a time to earn brownie points with the judges who tended to mark on the basis of a skater's reputation. Once again, Karen, with the pressure off, did not skate up to par. "She received, from charitable judges, points ranging from 5.4 to 5.7," wrote Ed Waring. Rick Matsumoto was blunter. "It didn't matter that Karen Magnussen fell twice and stumbled a third time during her free skating performance . . . She had the title all wrapped up long before she ever left her North Vancouver home and her performance here was just a formality. . . There was no one else capable of offering a serious challenge. After the compulsory figures she held a commanding lead. There's no denying that Miss Magnussen was protected by the fact she is Canada's main hope for a gold medal in the Winter Olympics . . . One well-respected figure skating expert admitted Karen received higher marks than she

Donald Jackson turned professional in 1962.

Donald Jackson gives a helping hand in the workshop where his line of skating boots is made *(below)*.

Donald McPherson turned professional with European Holiday on Ice after winning the world title in 1963. He is still training the show's skaters.

Petra Burka, 1963.

Petra Burka, aged 5, with sister *(above)*.

Petra Burka in show business, 1967 *(right)*.

Karen Magnussen, aged six, wearing her first $5 skates *(left)*.

Karen Magnussen signed for the Ice Capades for $300,000 in 1975 *(below)*.

Vern Taylor performed the world's first triple Axel in competition in 1978.

Sandra and Val Bezic won the World Professional Pairs Championships in 1980 *(above)*.

Tracey Wainman, right, in tears after losing her Canadian title in 1982. She is consoled by junior skater Tracey Robertson *(right)*.

Toller Cranston, 1975, brought a unique approach to modern skating.

**Barbara Underhill and Paul Martini in 1982. They won the world title
in Ottawa two years later.**

deserved, but in the next breath he added that this was the only way to protect Canada's chances for a gold medal in Sapporo. 'There is no way that Canada would send Miss Magnussen to the Olympics with anything less than the title of Canadian champion and with top marks in the nationals', he said.''

The games, opened by Emperor Hirohito, cost the Japanese seventeen million dollars to stage. Since the island race had been accustomed for many centuries to conserving space, the skating rink posed a particular problem. The ingenious engineers solved it by freezing over the swimming pool. How they did it was a bit of a mystery — Sheldon Galbraith actually walked along the bottom of the empty pool and gazed up at the large block of ice above him — but it served its purpose admirably even though the ice was three feet below the edge of the pool, and the skaters had to step down to perform.

Trixi Schuba won the gold and got her rightful cheers this time, but the interest in the skating world still focused on the two girls from North America. Karen, who halved Trixi's 141.3 lead after figures with a stunning free skate performance, got the silver, and Janet stood on the authentic podium to receive her bronze.

Shortly afterwards, Trixi turned professional, and Karen's route to the world crown was clear. Clear, that is, except for the challenge from Janet Lynn and the orchestrated American propaganda campaign.

There was another development that supporters of the two champions on either side of the border considered points in their respective heroine's favor. The International Skating Union had finally bowed to world pressure and the mighty army of armchair critics sitting in front of millions of T.V. sets, and once again changed the marking system so that the single's event would be a three part competition. In the first part, skaters would be required to perform three figures instead of six, and the figures would count for only forty percent of the total marks. Secondly, two minute compulsory free skating programme with prescribed free skating elements, would be worth twenty percent of the marks, and the final free skating programme, four minutes for women, and five minutes for men, would be worth the final forty percent. At last the balance had swung in favor of the talented free skater, but figures, the true basic of the sport, would still play an important role. It had also been decided that gold medals would be awarded separately for figures and for free skating.

With the North American Championships abandoned after 1971, the 1973 Canadian Championships were Karen's last chance to influence the World's judges. They were held in Vancouver, and the home crowd was expecting nothing but the best. Karen amassed a big lead in the figures, but in the free skating was outclassed by an up-and-coming sixteen-year old from Ottawa, Lynn Nightingale. Lynn edged Karen out of first place in the new compulsory free skate event, and was tied with the champion in the four-minute programme. "Miss Magnussen put on a fine free skating performance last night, but was overshadowed by a little-known Ottawa skater who brought the crowd to its feet with an outstanding programme," reported Canadian Press. "The question is whether Miss Magnussen's loss in free skating will adversely effect her chances in the world championship."

The American Championships were held a month after the Canadian's and Janet Lynn skated a first-class performance getting marks of three 6.0s and two 5.9s, which some thought were slightly exotic. They were certainly protective as her total points were less than two ahead of the runner-up, Dorothy Hamill. After showing Janet's full programme, the producers of ABC television showed the American public the kind of opposition she would be up against in the World's, using a brief clip of Karen's only fall during her Canadian performance, combined with some remarks from Dick Button that, as the Canadian champion was obviously not skating well, Janet Lynn's chances for the world title looked excellent.

"That's the way figure skating is," wrote Jim Proudfoot. "Psychological warfare is critical because points are based, in the final analysis, on the subjective opinions of nine very human judges and because, when you reach the level of a Karen or a Janet, the loser will be the girl who's just a shade below her best during the three days of competition."

The politicking continued right up to the day of competition in Bratislava. Karen was given little recognition in Europe for her latest title win, or her excellent bid for the top placement in the world. In England she was not invited to take part in a two-day gala at Queen's Ice Club in London, although Janet Lynn and Dorothy Hamill of the United States and Christine Errath of East Germany, all contenders for the crown, were invited to attend the televised show. Newspapers and magazines carried picture spreads of Janet Lynn, and the Championship brochures, while speculating on the new champion, made no reference at all to the Canadian girl.

"I guess they're trying to psyche me out," said Karen. "If they are, it's a mistake because all they are doing is firing me up." She was fired up enough to take an early lead in the compulsory figures, although the judges marked Janet close behind her in points. But Karen received the essential ordinals, eight first place and one second, and Canada had won its first gold medal of the championships.

In the short compulsory, she skated a strong controlled programme to Lalo's Scherzo, and competently completed all the required elements, a double Axel, a flying change-jump sit spin, a delayed single Axel, a combination Lutz-double cherry. She received marks ranging from 5.7 (the U.S. and Hungarian judges) to 5.9 (Canadian and British judges) for technical merit, and four 5.7s, four 5.8s, and one 5.9 for artistic impression. Good marks, but still capable of being topped by Janet Lynn. In the way of judges, they were "leaving room" for the next major contender. However flawless they may have considered Karen's performance, they knew that the American champion had received higher marks in recent competition, even though the marks had been awarded by American judges. Those waiting to see a good fierce competition between the two girls were destined for disappointment, as Janet Lynn virtually eliminated herself from a chance at the gold by skating clumsily and falling twice in the short programme. One of the falls was during the double Axel, and the other on the jump combination which included a double Axel. She had flubbed one of the most important jumps in the programme. In the end, by the complexity of the points system, she came out with a total of 96.9 points to Karen's 104.1, a narrow enough difference considering the disparity between a flawless performance and one that was badly marred.

From Karen came nothing but sympathy. "I wanted to beat Janet, but on a day when both of us would have skated well. That would have made for a good fight. It was unfortunate that she had a bad day."

In Karen's free skating long programme, the drama of the moment was heightened by her striking hotpink outfit, and the music, Rachmaninoff's Symphony No. 2. in E minor. In spite of her narrow lead she threw herself whole-heartedly into her carefully choreographed programme — camel turns, flying camel, flying sit-spin, double Axel, double Lutz and combinations. "She just didn't hold back, although she could have, and that's one of the key reasons that she won," said Donald Jackson. "Her programme was absolutely flawless, and after the double Axel there was no question that she had the title in her pocket. Halfway through the four minute programme when the mood changed to the composer's third piano concerto, she knew she had won it."

She completed the programme with a graceful layback spin, and the crowd rose, knowing even before the marks, that she would be the new champion. For technical merit she earned four 5.8s and five 5.9s. For artistic impression, three 5.8s and six 5.9s. "When I went out on the ice, I wasn't nervous at all, but I was determined to do well and not be cautious. What I did was to skate my usual programme to the best of my ability, and it really paid off."

Even though Janet Lynn came back to skate a splendid routine that earned her two perfect 6.0s for composition and style, she couldn't score enough to catch up.

Lynn Nightingale also impressed the crowd with her free skating, particularly in performing two double Axels in a row, coming tenth overall. Toller Cranston, who had won the free skating in the previous World's and had the best performance in the current compulsory programme, fell while attempting a triple jump and ended fifth behind defending champion Ondrej Nepela of Czechoslovakia, Sergei Chetverukhin of the Soviet Union, Jan Hoffman of East Germany, and John Curry of Britain. "I don't like making excuses," Cranston said. "I can't say it was the pressure or the ice conditions. I didn't come up with the goods. I have no excuses. I simply had a bad day."

Karen completed a world championship tour and returned to Vancouver for the biggest series of receptions for a Canadian skater since Barbara Ann Scott won her Olympic medal in 1948. At the airport she was met by the premier of British Columbia, Dave Barrett, and then rode in a motorcade to the cheers of thousands. A few days later, 15,711 people paid one dollar each to attend her birthday party at the Pacific National Exhibition, with the money going to a bursary fund set up in her name. "It was the best birthday present of all,'' she said, ''because it will make possible the development of promising young skaters who may, one day, bring more skating titles to Canada.''

Rumors were rife about her turning professional, and right up until the last minute the American propaganda on behalf of their Janet continued. ''She won't give up before she has a world title, which she is bound to get next year,'' said one official. ''Miss Magnussen, on the other hand, would have nothing to gain but everything to lose in case of reappearance next year.''

Vancouver's Cinderella ended the speculation by signing a $300,000 three-year contract with the Ice Capades, the largest it had ever offered a skater. For Canada, it closed the door on the Golden Age. Karen's medal would be the last gold won in international competition until 1984.

**Toller Cranston, the outspoken, controversial
artist/skater from Lachine, Quebec.**

21

The Fallow Years

The decade between the golds were years complete with drama, intrigue, disillusionment, endeavor, and politics. Only the names, and sometimes the locations, changed.

Toller Cranston, the extroverted introvert, the outspoken, controversial artist/skater from Lachine, Quebec, was never beatified by the international judges, yet he gained more attention for himself than many who had a crop of world medals hanging in the study. As he himself claims, he had more than a passing affinity with Jackson Haines, who had outraged the skating establishment a hundred years before. In his book "Toller" he says:

> "I have been called the pioneer of artistic skating, and although I actually don't like that description, I know what people mean. The true pioneer, however, of my kind of skating was the man now known as the father of modern figure skating — Jackson Haines. He was a hundred years ahead of his time, a great skater, and a fabulous performer in every sense of the word. Like so many pathfinders he was bitterly resented, and only a handful of people could appreciate and understand what he was trying to do. Strangely, on the night before he died, he wrote, "I predict a hundred years will pass before my dreams for artistic skating will come to be realized." He died

in Finland in 1879*. He gave to the world the founda-
tions of creative skating, yet few people know his
name. There are so many parallels between myself
and the man, that sometimes I believe I am his reincarnation. Like me he was born in Canada; he was
misunderstood, ridiculed and stifled. He too was a
painter. I feel more and more that I am tied to him by
a bond that transcends time — that, should I ever
meet him, I would know him well.''

Hyperbole, insight, self-pity, salesmanship? Toller, never at a
loss for words, was always a delight to the thousands who watched
his spectacular performances, a thorn in the side to many of the
establishment figures at a loss to understand his constant sniping
and apparent eagerness to be quoted, a source of controversy
among skating experts and, above all, an enigma — perhaps even
to himself. After a dinner in Ottawa, he was once quoted by the
Canadian Press as not wishing to be "classified," either as a person or a skater.

As a skater he cannot be ignored. He reigned as Canadian
champion for six successive years, 1971-76. In 1974 he placed third
in the World's winning the bronze, and won the gold medal for
free skating. In 1975 he again won the free skating gold, and in
1976 the free skating silver. The same year he received the bronze
medal at the Innsbruck Olympics.

Throughout his skating career he supported himself with pro-
ceeds from the sale of his paintings, as controversial as his skating.
As recently as June 1984, art critic Christopher Hume wrote in the
Toronto Star:

"There are artists, and there are skaters, and then
there is Toller Cranston.
The fabulous Toller, known primarily for his athletic
prowess, has returned with an exhibition of recent
paintings, prints and drawings . . . . The show is vin-
tage Cranston, which means mostly large, im-
maculately painted pretty pictures.

*Haines died of pneumonia in January 1876 after being
caught in a snowstorm while enroute by sleigh from St
Petersburg to Stockholm. He was buried in the little Fin-
nish town of Gamla-Karleby, where a granite monument
was raised by the people of Finland.

He calls his works "windows." Through them we glimpse a fantasy world inhabited by unicorns, butterflies and multi-colored damsels.

With more than seventy pieces on display, the show offers a complete survey of what Toller does when he's not in skates. 'I work like a demon,' says Toller . . . . 'but skating has definitely cramped my style as an artist.'

Judging from the look of these endlessly fussy and effeminate paintings, Toller's style could stand to be cramped a whole lot more than it has been. But in his case, style becomes the man.

'I'm a really good painter,' Toller says matter-of-factly. He's right.

Unfortunately technique, no matter how good, does not an artist make. His works look like something Aubrey Beardsley might have done if he'd worked for Hallmark Cards."

It was not the first time Cranston had been assailed by the slings and arrows of outraged critics nor would it be the last. He always appeared to take it in his stride, however, and with his facility for words, usually gave back as good as he got and often a little more quickly.

In February 1972, he finished ninth in his first Winter Olympics, which took place in Sapporo, Japan. Later, he told Dick Beddoes of the Globe and Mail: "Anyone who equates figure skating rationally realizes that taking it seriously is the first step to entering an asylum. It is an expensive practical joke."

He was expressing his ire at the judging. "The skating itself is not a joke. The joke is the actual officiating, which is incomprehensible to any rational person. When you're coming up the ladder like I am, you can't afford to make a mistake. To reach the top, you must spend many years proving yourself at the botton."

The underlying truth of his comments did not endear him to the international judging fraternity. Neither did his outspoken comments on the romantic tangles in the Russian camp build him future marks from East bloc judges. He told Beddoes: "It's pretty well known about the affairs of the Russian pairs. The No. 2 Soviet pair, Ludmila Smirnova and Andrei Souraikin, were lovers until this season. The Russians like their pairs to be lovers. Then Ludmila and Andrei fell out, and she began dating the boy on the No. 1 Soviet pair, Alexei Ulanov. The Russian officials didn't like that situation.''

When the same Alexei Ulanov and his partner Irina Rodnina beat the second Russian pair for the gold medal by one point, Cranston maintained that the second pair was shipped home immediately.

The next year, at the Bratislava World Championships, much of Cranston's story was borne out when Miss Rodnina appeared with a new partner, Alexander Zaitsev, whom she later married, and Ulanov was paired, on the ice as well as off, with the former Miss Smirnova, now his wife.

Part of what made Toller outrageous to the skating establishment was that he said right out loud what others only thought. ''Why should Canadians scream when we don't get medals?'' he would often ask. ''We don't need the public's support when we're on the podium. We need it when we're climbing the ladder.''

In Bratislava, Cranston was the favorite of the crowd. People were already on their feet clapping and roaring just for his warm-up for the compulsories. They were ecstatic when he won after a dazzling display. While his coach Ellen Burka beamed with pride, Alain Calmat, former French world champion and now a judge noted: ''Artistically, he was superb and totally original. No one can do what Toller can do on the ice. His combined technique and artistic approach is wonderful. He is the one man who has at last combined sport and art in skating.'' Then came Toller's fatigue fall in the long programme, which put him out of contention for any medals.

When he won his free skating titles in the World's, he was described by the European press as ''the skater of the century.'' At home, he had a comparatively cool reception, like many of the skaters before him. Like them, he lamented, ''As a skater I would never have been as successful as I am had I not made it outside the country first.''

Cranston skated his last amateur performance at the 1976 Olympics, and a Toronto writer's prediction of a year earlier came true. ''Gold medals, after all, go to winners, not to artists.'' In the figures, Toller's marks were as low as 3.3 (from the French judge), but doing what he does best, he was top in the short programme and second best in the free skating, earning a third-place bronze. Not unnaturally, he didn't revere the "figure" part of figure skating. "Figures are a lot of crap. . . . The way skating is evolving, figures just aren't a part of what is happening. . . Let figures die their natural death." He turned professional, taking his unique style into the atmosphere of dramatic showmanship where it seemed to belong.

At the same Olympics, Ron Shaver, who had long skated in the shadow of Toller Cranston, had solid performances in the figures and the compulsory, but injured a groin in practice and had to withdraw. A year later, he succeeded to the Canadian title, came sixth in the World's in Tokyo, and immediately turned professional. With him went four-time Canadian champion Lynn Nightingale, who finished eighth at the World's.

Two years before, Canada's best hope for a pair's medal, Sandra and Val Bezic, had left amateur competition as well. They had first won the Canadian title in 1970, and over a period of five years had gradually improved their world standing from fourteenth to fifth. Their target, said Sandra, was the 1976 Olympics, but in 1975 she suffered a thyroid problem, and their amateur skating career was over. After a long battle against the metabolic upset, the pair returned to skating as pros, and in 1980 won the World's Professional Championships.

With Cranston, Shaver, Nightingale and the Bezics turning professional, Canada entered the skating doldrums, and newspapers, instead of talking about the glitter of gold, ran headlines like, "No Hope of Medals for Canadians."

In 1978, the World Championships were held in Ottawa. The thought brought despair to Toronto Star writer, Jim Proudfoot. He understood why Shaver and Nightingale had joined a professional show because, "Shaver was fifth in the world three seasons ago, and Nightingale sixth the same year. They're slipping badly at a time when they should be gaining ground. Now, all the Ottawa folks will have to sell in 1978 is in the doubles competition. Toronto dancers Susan Carscallen and Eric Gillies were Canada's best in Tokyo — a very commendable sixth. And juniors Sherri Baier and Robin Cowan made an impressive debut finishing tenth. The trouble is that the Soviet Union is simply invincible in both categories."

He went on to outline the problem that had faced Toller Cranston:

"Invariably, Canada's skaters get so far behind in the school figures that even brilliant free skating can't rescue them. Yet there's nothing especially difficult about figures. All they require is a lot of practice. It's an old saying in skating, and a true one, that as long as you cover enough miles, you'll come out on top. If athletes don't do figures properly, it's because they haven't trained enough or haven't been taught correctly. Canada has more skaters than any other nation. That's a statistical fact. The law of averages says we should be getting more medals than we do."

Glib though some of the statements may have been, they carried enough truth to concern all who had the best interests of skating at heart. However, a suggestion by one International Skating Union president that figures should be eliminated from world competition, brought strong negative reactions from coaches, skaters and former champions.

On the Canadian scene, there were occasional flashes of hope. Vern Taylor, studying with Sheldon Galbraith, won the 1973 novice title at the age of fourteen completing the first triple Lutz done in national or international competition since Donald Jackson had astounded the world in 1962. Taylor went on to perform the world's first triple Axel in competition at the World's championship in 1978. But before he could reach his potential as an amateur, he too turned professional.

Then there was Tracey Wainmann, an appealing young prodigy who succumbed to pressures largely inflicted by those who should have known better. Tracey first came to public attention in 1980 when Heather Kemkaran, an attractive, dark-haired, 21-year-old, won the Canadian title. She had trained fiercely to get back the title she had won in 1978, then narrowly lost again in 1979 to Janet Morissey, and had fought a personal battle to regain her form. A week after winning her title back, she was informed by the C.F.S.A. that she would not be representing Canada in the World's at Lake Placid, New York. The honor was going to the third-place finisher, twelve-year-old Tracey Wainmann. The reason given by the official body was that Tracey, regarded as future championship material, would be affected by an upward change in the ISU age rules if she did not compete in 1980. "It was a real insult to me,'' said Heather. ''I couldn't see the reason.'' Both skaters at the time were taught by Ellen Burka.

Tracey skated to tenth place in the World Championships, won the Canadian title in 1981, and was deposed a year later by Kay Thomson of Toronto, who remained champion until she turned pro in 1984. The Canadian Figure Skating Association, criticized by many for their decision in 1980, came under further fire as the young ''skating phenomenon'' faded from contention. Many quoted a government-sponsored study which showed that talented kids were just that. The controversy, now muted, continues as young Tracey, an attractive and warm schoolgirl, fights to come to grips with the pressures of growing up, of being a deposed champion, and of being the torch bearer for the expectations of so many others.

Canada's skating hopes had sunk so low that in 1980, under a headline stating, ''Canadian Figure Skaters Won't Win Any Medals,'' Jack Lynch, technical co-ordinator of the Canadian Olympic Association said, ''It's remotely possible that Dowding and Wighton (Canadian dance pair, ranked sixth in the world) will be the only ones we'll send to the Lake Placid Olympics.''

In the end, a team was sent which included Barbara Underhill and Paul Martini, twice Canadian pairs champions, who finished ninth. But in the meantime the concern with the overall standard of skating continued. Barbara Graham, international judge and technical co-ordinator of the Canadian Figure Skating Association, commented on the failure of Canadians to do well in the compulsory figures. ''School figures require concentration and discipline which come from dedicated training,'' she said. ''Those are not qualities you usually find in Canadian society today. If Canadians insist on playing catch-up skating (free style) they are not going to be on the podium.''

Kerry Leitch, head coach of the Preston Figure Skating Club said, ''There is a different attitude among kids today. Youngsters are not as disciplined as they used to be in the home and school.'' He felt that youngsters were willing to accept discipline and could cope with demands. ''Our job is to encourage parents to take the same route regarding discipline that we do, in their handling of discipline at home.'' He was to demonstrate his point in the summer of 1984, when one pupil who broke ranks was given the choice of running twenty-five miles, or missing out on an overseas trip and competition. He ran.

In the meantime, in the face of general agreement that more good coaches were needed and more work had to be done on figures, Garry Beacom, the 1977 junior champion and himself potential star material, expressed the view that there was more depth in Canadian skating than there had been in recent years. "The potential has not been witnessed yet," he said.

It was not until 1982 that his predictions began to come true, when three time Canadian champion Brian Pockar of Calgary, coached by Winnie Silverthorne, won a bronze medal in world competition. The next year, after Pockar turned professional, Brian Orser of Orillia won a bronze in the World Championships, and Underhill and Martini were judged out of the silver, but took the bronze. Canada was back on the podium, and the bad years were behind.

Tears of joy from Barbara Underhill, as she and her partner Paul Martini win the Gold Medal in the 1984 World Championships in Ottawa.

22

Ice Gold

Success came early to Barbara Underhill and Paul Martini and they showed all the potential for being the golden boy and girl of the era, but in the end it was a pair of old boots that propelled them to the top.

Like Canada's greatest pairs couple, Wagner and Paul, the first North American pair to win, in 1960, an Olympic gold medal, they had not started out with the intention of becoming a pair. Also, like their predecessors, there was a substantial height difference. Both had achieved some success with other partners, but were still taking singles coaching, Underhill with Louis Stong at Weston Summer School and Martini with Judy Henderson. Stong felt that with their previous background they might make a good pair and suggested they skate a few practice laps around the arena. His original impression was that Barbara, at five feet, was too short for Paul — an athletic six-footer — but he and Henderson both felt that with proper choreography the height difference could be overcome.

They spent the rest of the summer skating together under Stong, and in the fall returned to a two coach system, Martini with Judy Henderson in Woodbridge, and Underhill with Anna Forder McLaughlin in Oshawa with André Denis doing the choreography. It was a long cry from the days when one coach was trainer, psychologist, choreographer and manager, but however unwieldy the system appeared to be in 1978, they had a rush of successes. First the Canadian junior title, followed by the World

Championship junior title in Megeve, France. In the short programme, with forty percent of the points, they had been placed fourth behind strong entries from the U.S.S.R., Czechoslovakia, and the United States, but decided to go for broke and knock the American pair, Beth and Ken Flora, out of second place. As a result, they skated so strongly that they ended up taking the title. Then they had a couple of first place finishes in two of the international championships which had sprung up in the early 1970s; The Grand Prix International in St. Gervais, France, and the Nebelthorn Trophy in Oberstdorf, West Germany. They also obtained a fifth place finish in their first major senior competition — the Ennia Challenge Cup in Holland.

The split-training system continued until the spring of 1979, when both skaters decided to train with Louis Stong, who had first suggested the partnership and had a track record of success with former Canadian Senior Pair's champions, Don Fraser and Candy Jones, who had won the titles in 1975 and 1976. Sandra Bezic and her brother Val, five-time Canadian champions, were persuaded to do the choreography, and later Sandra was to become joint coach.

In 1979, they won their first national senior title, and successfully defended it in 1980. "The Canadian championships are probably the toughest competitions that we go to," said Barbara. "When you are the champion, everyone is out to get you. At other competitions, we're trying to get somebody else." The same year, 1980, they earned a satisfying ninth place in the Lake Placid Winter Olympics, but were disappointed at their eleventh place finish in the World's at Dortmund.

By 1983, they had come up enough to gain a third place finish at the World Championships in Helsinki, and win the first medal given to a Canadian pair since 1964 when Debbie Wilkes and Gary Revell finished third in the World's and took the silver medal at the Olympics in Innsbruck. Their progress to the top three in the world was marked by their graceful team work and ability to execute dangerous moves, opening the programme with a triple twist which sent Underhill flying through the air for three spins. But while their technical expertise could not be challenged, they had marred some of their performances in international competition by missing some of the simplest moves in their programme. After Helsinki, they decided to take a rest from international competition for a while. "We thought this would inject an element of anticipation into our Olympic appearance," said Martini.

A pulled ligament in Martini's ankle the month before the Canadian Championships in 1984, convinced the couple not to defend their title, and instead spend time working on their Olympic programme at Toronto's Granite Club. In the absence of their two coaches, Stong and Bezic, who were at the championships, Sheldon Galbraith was called in to help bring the couple back to their competitive peak. Although they thought that rest and training would put them on top, they were later to regret the lack of tournament practice when they competed in the 1984 Winter Olympics at Sarajevo.

"I'm going back to my room for a good cry," was what Barbara said at a press conference following the completion of their short programme at the Olympics, and the words said it all. She had suffered a disastrous fall when backing into a simple sit spin, and Martini had come tumbling after her. The fall had ruined their performance, placed them sixth, and effectively put them out of contention for the gold medal. The pair from the Soviet Union, Elena Valova and Oleg Vasiliev, had skated flawlessly and were way out in front, and only a similar disaster could stop them from winning the event. Norris Bowden, himself no stranger to Olympic disappointment, still saw some success for the Canadian pair. "If they could win the free skating final or come second, there's still a chance they'll get a medal. They're certainly capable of doing it but the problem is going to be psychological." For the young hopefuls there was not only the memory of that fall on one of the simplest mandatory movements, but the memory of accidents with similar routines which had cost them dearly in two previous world championships. Only in Helsinki had they been at their impeccable best, where many thought they were unfortunate not to have been placed second.

"I feel awfully bad right now, but we'll sit down tomorrow and think the whole thing over and get our confidence built up again. It's a pretty low point for sure, but we've been through this kind of thing before. What's happened may seem like the end of the world but we'll get it back into perspective in a hurry." Those were brave words for Barbara Underhill under the inquisitorial media spotlights that top athletes, even when they lose, have to face after major competition. But alone with her thoughts, and with twenty-four hours to go before the next appearance on ice, the twenty-year-old found the pressures almost too much to bear. She sought the company of coach Sandra Bezic. "We walked the village and cried together," said Sandra. "But after five or six hours I took her to see the team chief medical examiner."

The tension of both skaters showed on their faces as they moved out to skate their final performance to Gene Krupa's Sing, Sing, Sing, and Gershwins's Piano Concerto in F. They skated a lackluster performance and placed seventh. The title went to Elena Valova and Oleg Vasiliev of the Soviet Union, followed by Kitty and Peter Carruthers of the United States, and Larissa Selezneva and Oleg Makarov also of the U.S.S.R.

"When I look back over the whole thing," said Martini, "I can only say it just wasn't meant for us to be here. Going in, I thought we were about as upbeat as we could possibly be, but two throws and one jump later, after we blew them all, we were in plenty of trouble."

Back in Toronto the couple returned to the Granite Club to try and polish their programme for the World Championships in Ottawa. On home territory, they would have their best chance ever of winning the gold, but the spark seemed to have gone. After an exhibition performance before a knowledgeable crowd at the Toronto Cricket Skating and Curling Club, when they fluffed simple moves and demonstrated increasing tension, they were at their lowest ebb. The next day they considered withdrawing from the World's and turning pro, as they had planned before the Olympics, but their coaches persuaded them to give it just one more try. In desperation, Barbara, who had been skating in new boots for several weeks, dug out an old pair of skates, gouged with blade marks from hundreds of hours of work on the ice. As soon as she put them on, the magic and her confidence returned — just in time. The couple skated to second place in the short programme behind the Olympic champions, then blazed ahead in the long programme to overtake the leaders and clinch the title. Fifteen seconds before the end, the crowd at the Ottawa Civic Centre began a standing ovation that lasted until long after the skaters had finished. "At first I thought the roof was coming down on us," said Underhill. "When I saw everybody standing on their feet, I thought, 'concentrate, concentrate.' It was a very special feeling. I've never experienced a thrill like that, having all those people cheering." And then the wait for the marks. They received one 5.7, six 5.8s and two 5.9s for technical merit, and two 5.7s, two 5.8s and five 5.9s for artistic impression. And once again, the tears of Barbara Underhill and Sandra Bezic mingled, but this time they were tears of joy marking the end of the trail to the top.

Two other Canadians finished in the top ten, Katherine Matousek and John Eisler, fifth, and Cynthia Coull and Mark Rowsom, tenth. And as final confirmation that Canada was once again on the move, Brian Orser repeated his Olympic silver medal performance, outskated the American title holder Scottie Hamilton in the free skate, and earned his second silver medal of the month.

Martini and Underhill turned professional, but Brian Orser, the other Canadian pairs, the Canadian dance champions, Tracy Wilson and Robert McCall, who have steadily been ascending the international ladder behind the now retired incomparable Torvill and Dean, are all still in the running for future world and Olympic honors.

A new age of gold could be just ahead.

Appendix

World Championship Medals
Won By Canadians

Year	Event	Name	1st	2nd	3rd
1930	W	Cecil Smith		S	
1932	M	Montgomery Wilson		S	
	W	Constance Samuel		S	
1947	W	Barbara Ann Scott	G		
1948	W	Barbara Ann Scott	G		
	P	Suzanne Morrow/Wallace Distelmeyer			B
1953	P	Frances Dafoe/Norris Bowden		S	
1954	P	Frances Dafoe/Norris Bowden	G		
1955	P	Frances Dafoe/Norris Bowden	G		
1956	P	Frances Dafoe/Norris Bowden		S	
1957	P	Barbara Wagner/Robert Paul	G		
	P	Maria Jelinek/Otto Jelinek			B
	D	Geraldine Fenton/William McLachlan		S	
	M	Charles Snelling			B
1958	P	Barbara Wagner/Robert Paul	G		
	P	Maria Jelinek/Otto Jelinek			B
	D	Geraldine Fenton/William McLachlan		S	
1959	P	Barbara Wagner/Robert Paul	G		
	M	Donald Jackson		S	
	D	Geraldine Fenton/William McLachlan			B
1960	P	Barbara Wagner/Robert Paul	G		
	P	Maria Jelinek/Otto Jelinek		S	
	M	Donald Jackson		S	
	D	Virginia Thompson/William McLachlan		S	
1962	M	Donald Jackson	G		
	P	Maria Jelinek/Otto Jelinek	G		
	W	Wendy Griner		S	
	D	Virginia Thomson/William McLachlan			B
1963	M	Donald McPherson	G		
	D	Paulette Doan/Kenneth Ormsby			B
1964	D	Paulette Doan/Kenneth Ormsby		S	
	W	Petra Burka			B
	P	Debbie Wilkes/Guy Revell			B
1965	W	Petra Burka	G		
	M	Donald Knight			B
1966	W	Petra Burka			B
1971	W	Karen Magnussen			B

1972	W	Karen Magnussen		S	
1973	W	Karen Magnussen	G*		
1974	M	Toller Cranston			B**
1982	M	Brian Pockar			B
1983	M	Brian Orser			B
	P	Barbara Underhill/Paul Martini			B
1984	P	Barbara Underhill/Paul Martini	G		
	M	Brian Orser		S	

* Also won gold medals for figures and free skating.
**Won free skating gold medals in 1974 and 1975, silver in 1976.

M = Men's   W = Women's   P = Pairs   D = Dance

Olympic Medals

Year	Event	Name	1st	2nd	3rd
1932	M	Montgomery Wilson			B
1948	W	Barbara Ann Scott	G		
	P	Suzanne Morrow/Wallace Distelmeyer			B
1956	P	Frances Dafoe/Norris Bowden		S	
1960	P	Barbara Wagner/Robert Paul	G		
	M	Donald Jackson			B
1964	P	Debbie Wilkes/Guy Revell		S	
	W	Petra Burka			B
1972	W	Karen Magnussen		S	
1976	M	Toller Cranston			B
1984	M	Brian Orser		S	

Canadian Championships

Year	Men's	Women's	Pairs	Dance
1905	Ormond Haycock	Anne Ewan	Katherine & Ormond Haycock	No competition (1905-1909)
1906	Ormond Haycock	Aimee Haycock	Katherine & Ormond Haycock	
1907	No competition	Minto Club burned down	No competition	
1908	Ormond Haycock	Aimee Haycock	Aimee & Ormond Haycock	
1909				
1910	D.H. Nelles	Iris Mudge	Lady Evelyn Grey/Ormond Haycock	
1911	Ormond Haycock	Lady Evelyn Grey	Lady Evelyn Grey/Ormond Haycock	Lady Evelyn Grey/Dudley Oliver Senior Waltz
1912	D.H. Nelles	Eleanor Kingsford	Eleanor Kingsford/Douglas Nelles	No competition (1911-1935)
1913	Phil Crysler	Eleanor Kingsford	Muriel Burrows/Gordon McLennan	
1914	Norman Scott	Muriel Maunsell	Jeanne Chevalier/Norman Scott	
1915-1919	No competition due to war			
1920	Norman Scott	Jeanne Chevalier	Alden Godwin/Douglas Nelles	
1921	Duncan Hodgson	Jeanne Chevalier	Beatrice MacDougall/Allan Howard	
1922	Duncan Hodgson	Dorothy Jenkins	Alden Godwin/Major AC Maclennan	
1923	Melville Rogers	Dorothy Jenkins	Majorie Annabel/Duncan Hodgson	
1924	John Machado	Constance Wilson	Elizabeth Blair/John Machado	
1925	Melville Rogers	Cecil Smith	Gladys & Melville Rogers	
1926	Melville Rogers	Cecil Smith	Constance Wilson/Errol Morson	
1927	Melville Rogers	Constance Wilson	Marion McDougall/Chauncey Bangs	
1928	Melville Rogers	Margot Barclay	Marion McDougall/Chauncey Bangs	
1929	Montgomery Wilson	Constance Wilson	Constance & Montgomery Wilson	
1930	Montgomery Wilson	Constance Wilson	Constance & Montgomery Wilson	
1931	Montgomery Wilson	Constance Wilson	Frances Claudet & Chauncey Bangs	
1932	Montgomery Wilson	Constance Samuel	Constance Samuel/Montgomery Wilson	
1933	Montgomery Wilson	Constance Samuel	Constance Samuel/Montgomery Wilson	
1934	Montgomery Wilson	Constance Samuel	Constance Samuel/Montgomery Wilson	
1935	Montgomery Wilson	Constance Samuel	Louise Bertram/Stewart Reburn	
1936	Osborne Colson	Eleanor O'Meara	Veronica Clarke/Ralph McCreath	Mr & Mrs Don Cruickshank Waltzing / Veronica Clarke/Jack Eastwood Tenstep

Year	Men	Ladies	Pairs	Dance
1937	Osborne Colson	Dorothy Caley	Veronica Clarke/Ralph McCreath	Mr & Mrs Don Cruickshank — Waltzing Veronica Clarke/Ralph McCreath — Tenstep
1938	Montgomery Wilson	Eleanor O'Meara	Veronica Clarke/Ralph McCreath	Janet & Fraser Sweatman — Waltzing Veronica Clarke/Ralph McCreath — Tenstep
1939	Montgomery Wilson	Mary Rose Thacker	Norah McCarthy/Ralph McCreath	Mr & Mrs Don Cruickshank — Waltzing Janet & Fraser Sweatman — Tenstep
1940	Ralph McCreath	Norah McCarthy	Norah McCarthy/Ralph McCreath	Mr & Mrs Don Cruickshank — Waltzing Mrs Elmore Davis/Melville Rogers — Tenstep
1941	Ralph McCreath	Mary Rose Thacker	Eleanor O'Meara/Ralph McCreath	Helen Malcolm!FKJ Geisler — Waltzing Norah McCarthy/Sandy McKechnie — Tenstep
1942	Michael Kirby	Mary Rose Thacker	Eleanor O'Meara/Sandy McKechnie	Eleanor O'Meara/Sandy McKechnie — Waltzing Evelyn Rogers/George McCullough — Tenstep
1943	No senior competition due to war			
1944	No event due to war	Barbara Ann Scott Marilyn Ruth Take Nadine Phillips	No Pairs or Dance due to war	
1945	Nigel Stephens Frank Sellers	Barbara Ann Scott Marilyn Ruth Take Nadine Phillips	Olga Bernyk/Alex Fulton	Gloria Lillico/William de Nance Jr. (Waltz) Olga Bernyk/Alex Fulton — Tenstep
1946 Schumaker	Ralph McCreath	Barbara Ann Scott Marilyn Ruth Take	Joyce Perkins/Wallace Distelmeyer	Gloria Lillico/William de Nance Jr. (Waltz) Marnie Brereton/Richard McLaughlin — Tenstep
1947 Toronto	Norris Bowden Wallace Distelmeyer Gerrard Blair	Marilyn Ruth Take Nadine Phillips Suzanne Morrow	Suzanne Morrow/Wallace Distelmeyer Margaret Roberts/Bruce Hyland	Margaret Roberts/Bruce Hyland Joyce Perkins/William de Nance Jr. Marnie Brereton/Richard McLaughlin

Year / City				
1948 Calgary	Wallace Distelmeyer Roger Wickson	Barbara Ann Scott Jeanne Matthews Marlene Smith	Suzanne Morrow/Wallace Distelmeyer Sheila & Ross Smith	Suzanne Morrow/Wallace Distelmeyer (Waltz)
1949 Ottawa	Roger Wickson William Evan Lewis Donald Tobin	Suzanne Morrow Patsy Earl Jeanne Matthews	Marlene Smith/Donald Gilchrist Pearle Simmers/David Spalding Joyce Perkins/Bruce Hyland	Joyce Perkins/Bruce Hyland (Silver Dance) Pierrette Paquin/Donald Tobin (Foxtrot)
1950 St. Catharines	Roger Wickson Donald Tobin William Lewis	Suzanne Morrow Marlene Smith Vevi Smith	Marlene Smith/Donald Gilchrist	Frances Dafoe/Norris Bowden (Waltz) Joy Forsyth/William de Nance Jr. (Foxtrot)
1951 Vancouver	Peter Firstbrook Roger Wilson William Lewis	Suzanne Morrow Vevi Smith Jane Kirby	Jane Kirby/Donald Tobin Frances Dafoe/Norris Bowden Gayle Wakely/David Spalding	Pierrette Paquin/Donald Tobin (Silver) Mary Trimble/David Ross (Tenstep) Frances Dafoe/Norris Bowden (Waltz)
1952 Oshawa	Peter Firstbrook William Lewis Peter Dunfield	Marlene Smith Vevi Smith Barbara Gratton	Frances Dafoe/Norris Bowden Audrey Downie/Brian Power	Frances Dafoe/Norris Bowden Joyce Kornacher/William de Nance Jr. Pierrette Paquin/Malcolm Wickson
1953 Ottawa	Peter Firstbrook Charles Snelling Peter Dunfield	Barbara Gratton Dawn Steckley Yarmila Pachl	Frances Dafoe/Norris Bowden Dawn Steckley/David Lowery	Frances Abbott/David Ross Patty Lou/George Montgomery Marian Wattie/Harry ball
1954 Calgary	Charles Snelling Douglas Court Paul Tatton	Barbara Gratton Sonja Currie Vevi Smith	Frances Dafoe/Norris Bowden Audrey Downie/Brian Power	Geraldine Fenton/William McLachlan Doreen Leech/Norman Wallace Claudette Lacaille/Jeffery Johnston
1955 Toronto	Charles Snelling Douglas Court	Carol Jane Pachl Ann Johnston Joan Shippam	Francis Dafoe/Norris Bowden Barbara Wagner/Robert Paul Audrey Downie/Brian Power	Lindis Johnston/Jeffery Johnston Geraldine Fenton/Gordon Crossland
1956 Galt	Charles Snelling Donald Jackson Douglas Court	Carol Pachl Ann Johnston Sonja Curril	Barbara Wagner/Robert Paul Maria Jelinek/Otto Jelinek Diane Neilson/Edwin Cossitt	Geraldine Fenton/William McLachlan Lindis Johnston/Jeffery Johnston Beverley de Nance/William de Nance
1957 Winnipeg	Charles Snelling Donald Jackson Edward Collins	Carol Pachl Karen Dixon Margaret Crosland	Barbara Wagner/Robert Paul Maria Jelinek/Otto Jelinek	Geraldine Fenton/William McLachlan Beverly Orr/Hugh Smith Elaine Protherol/William Trimble
1958 Ottawa	Charles Snelling Donald Jackson Edward Collins	Margaret Crosland Doreen Lister Sonia Snelling	Barbara Bourne/Tom Monypenny Barbara Wagner/Robert Paul Maria Jelinek/Otto Jelinek	Geraldine Fenton/William McLachlan Beverley Orr/Hugh Smith Svata Staroba/Mirek Staroba

Year / City				
1959 Noranda	Donald Jackson	Margaret Crosland	Barbara Wagner/Robert Paul	Geraldine Fenton/William McLachlan
	Edward Collins	Sonia Snelling	Jane Sinclair/Larry Rost	Ann Martin/Edward Collins
		Sandra Tewkesbury	Lise Petit/Ian Knight	Svata Staroba/Mirek Staroba
				Mary Jane Lennie/Karl Benzing
1960 Regina	Donald Jackson	Wendy Griner	Barbara Wagner/Robert Paul	Virginia Thompson/William McLachlan
	Donald McPherson	Shirra Kenworthy	Maria & Otto Jelinek	Donna & John Mitchell
	Louis Stong	Sonia Snelling	Debbie Wilkes/Guy Revell	Paulette Doan/Kenneth Ormsby
1961 Lachine	Donald Jackson	Wendy Griner	Maria Jelinek/Otto Jelinek	Virginia Thompson/William McLachlan
	Donald McPherson	Shirra Kenworthy	Gertrude Desjardins/Maurice Lafrance	Donna & John Mitchell
	Bradley Black	Sonia Snelling	Debbie Wilkes/Guy Revell	Marilyn Crawford/Blair Armitage
1962 Toronto	Donald Jackson	Wendy Griner	Maria & Otto Jelinek	Paulette Doan/Kenneth Ormsby
	Donald McPherson	Petra Burka	Gertrude Desjardins/Maurice Lafrance	Donna & John Mitchell
	Donald Knight	Shirra Kenworthy	Debbie Wilkes/Guy Revell	Carole Forrest/Kevin Lethbridge
1963 Edmonton	Donald McPherson	Wendy Griner	Debbie Wilkes/Guy Revell	Paulette Doan/Kenneth Ormsby
	Donald Knight	Petra Burka	Gertrude Desjardins/Maurice Lafrance	Carole Forrest/Kevin Lethbridge
	Gregory Folk	Valerie Jones	Linda Ward/Neil Carpenter	Marilyn Crawford/Blair Armitage
1964 North Bay	Dr. Charles Snelling	Petra Burka	Debbie Wilkes/Guy Revell	Carole Forrest/Kevin Lethbridge
	Donald Knight	Wendy Griner	Linda Ward/Neil Carpenter	Lynn Matthews/Bryan Topping
	Jay Humphrey	Shirra Kenworthy	Faye Stratt/Jim Watters	Gail Snyder/Wayne Palmer
1965 Calgary	Donald Knight	Petra Burka	Susan & Paul Huehnergard	Carole Forrest/Kevin Lethbridge
	Dr. Charles Snelling	Valerie Jones	Alexis & Chris Shields	Gail Snyder/Wayne Palmer
	Jay Humphry	Gloria Tatton	Faye Strutt/James Watters	Judy Henderson/John Bailey
1966 Peterborough	Donald Knight	Petra Burka	Susan & Paul Huehnergard	Joni Graham/Don Phillips
	Dr. Charles Snelling	Valerie Jones	Alexis & Chris Shields	Judy Henderson/John Bailey
	Jay Humphry	Roberta Laurent	Betty & John McKilligan	
1967 Toronto,	Donald Knight	Valerie Jones	Betty & John McKilligan	Maureen Peever/Wayne Palmer
	Jay Humphry	Karen Magnussen	Alexis & Chris Shields	Joni Graham/Don Phillips
	Dr. Charles Snelling	Roberta Laurent	Anna Forder/Rick Stephens	
1968 Vancouver	Jay Humphry	Karen Magnussen	Betty/John McKilligan	Donna Taylor/Bruce Lennie
	David McGillivray	Linda Carbonetto	Anna Forder/Richard Stephens	Mary Church/Tom Falls
	Steve Hutchinson	Lyndsai Cowan	Alexis/Chris Shields	
1969 Toronto	Jay Humphry	Linda Carbonetto	Anna Forder/Richard Stephens	Donna Taylor/Bruce Lennie
	David McGillivray	Karen Magnussen	Mary Petrie/Robert McAvoy	Mary Church/Tom Falls
	Toller Cranston	Cathy Lee Irwin	Sandra Bezic/Val Bezic	
1970 Edmonton	David McGillivray	Karen Magnussen	Sandra & Val Bezic	Hazel Pike/Phillip Boskill
	Paul Bonenfant		Mary Petrie/John Hubbell	Mary Church/David Sutton
	Toller Cranston			
1971 Winnipeg	Toller Cranston	Karen Magnussen	Sandra & Val Bezic	Louise Lind/Barry Soper
	Paul Bonenfant	Ruth Hutchinson	Mary Petrie/John Hubbell	Mary Church/David Sutton
	Kenneth Polk	Diane Hall	Marian Murray/Glenn Moore	Brenda Sandys/James Holden

Year / City

1972 London
1973 Vancouver
1974 Moncton
1975 Quebec
1976 London
1977 Calgary
1978 Victoria
1979 Thunder Bay
1980 Kitchener
1981 Halifax
1982 Brandon
1983 Montreal
1984 Regina

Men

Toller Cranston
Paul Bonenfant
Kenneth Polk
Toller Cranston
Ron Shaver
Robert Rubens
Toller Cranston
Ron Shaver
Robert Rubens
Toller Cranston
Bob Rubens
Stan Bohonek
Toller Cranston
Ron Shaver
Stan Bohonek
Ron Shaver
Brian Pockar
Vern Taylor
Brian Pockar
Vern Taylor
Jim Szabo
Brian Pockar
Vern Taylor
Gordon Forbes
Brian Pockar
Gordon Forbes
Gary Beacom
Brian Orser
Brian Pockar
Gordon Forbes
Brian Orser
Brian Pockar
Dennis Coi
Brian Orser
Gary Beacom
Gordon Forbes
Brian Orser
Gary Beacom
Gordon Forbes

Women

Karen Magnussen
Ruth Hutchinson
Cathy Lee Irwin
Karen Magnussen
Cathy Lee Irwin
Lynn Nightingale
Lynn Nightingale
Barbara Terpenning
Daria Prychun
Lynn Nightingale
Kim Alletson
Barbara Terpenning
Lynn Nightingale
Kim Alletson
Susan MacDonald
Lynn Nightingale
Heather Kemkaren
Kim Alletson
Heather Kemkaran
Cathie MacFarlane
Peggy McLean
Janet Morrissey
Heather Kemkaran
Deborah Albright
Heather Kemkaren
Janet Morrissey
Tracey Wainman
Tracey Wainman
Kay Thomson
Elizabeth Manley
Kay Thomson
Elizabeth Manley
Tracey Wainman
Kay Thomson
Charlene Wong
Cynthia Coull
Kay Thomson
Elizabeth Manley
Cynthia Coull

Pairs

Sandra & Val Bezic
Mary Petrie/John Hubbell
Linda Tasker/Allen Carson
Sandra & Val Bezic
Marian Murray/Glenn Moore
Linda Tasker/Allen Carson
Sandra & Val Bezic
Marian Murray/Glenn Moore
Kathy Hutchinson/Jamie McGrigor
Candy Jones/Donald Fraser
Kathy Hutchinson/Jamie McGrigor
Christine McBeth/Dennis Johnston
Candy Jones/Don Fraser
Cheri Pinner/Dennis Pinner
Karen Newton/Glen Laframboise
Cheri Pinner/Dennis Pinner
Sherri Baier/Robin Gowan
Lee-Ann Jackson/Paul Mills
Susan Gowan/Eric Thomsen
Barbara Underhill/Paul Martini
Susan Gowan/Eric Thomsen
Lee-Ann Jackson/Bernard Souche
Barbara Underhill/Paul Martini
Lorri Baier/Lloyd Eisler
Becky Gough/Mark Rowson
Barbara Underhill/Paul Martini
Lorrie Baier/Lloyd Eisler
Becky Gough/Mark Rowson
Barbara Underhill/Paul Martini
Lorrie Baier/Lloyd Eisler
Becky Gough/Mark Rowson
Barbara Underhill/Paul Martini
Cynthia Coull/Mark Rowson
Katherina Matousek/Lloyd Eisler
Melinda Kunhegyi/Lyndon Johnston
Cynthia Coull/Mark Rowson

Dance

Louise Lind/Barry Soper
Barbara Berezowski/David Porter
Linda Roe/Michael Bradley
Louise Soper/Barry Soper
Barbara Berezowski/David Porter
Lind Roe/Michael Bradley
louise Soper/Barry Soper
Barbara Berezowski/David Porter
Lind Roe/Michael Bradley
Barbara Berezowski/David Porter
Susan Carscallen/Eric Gillies
Shelley MacLeod/Bob Knapp
Barbara Berezowski/David Porter
Susan Carscallen/Erric Gillies
Lorna Wighton/John Dowding
Susan Carscallen/Erric Gillies
Lorna Wighton/John Dowding
Debbie Young/Greg Young
Lorna Wighton/John Dowding
Patricia Fletcher/Michael De La Penotiere
Marie McNeil/Robert McCall
Lorna Wighton/John Dowding
Patricia Fletcher/Michael De La Penotiere
Marie McNeil/Robert McCall
Lorna Wighton/John Dowding
Marie McNeil/Robert McCall
Gina Aucoin/Peter Ponikau
Marie McNeil/Robert McCall
Kelly Johnson/Kris Barber
Joanne French/John Thomas
Tracy Wilson/Robert McCall
Kelly Johnson/Kris Barbara
Joanne French/John Thomas
Tracy Wilson/Robert McCall
Kelly Johnson/John Thomas
Karyn Carossino/Rod Carossino
Tracy Wilson/Robert McCall
Kelly Johnson/John Thomas
Karyn Carossino/Rod Carossino

Photo Credits
David Bell
Sandra Bezik
Norris Bowden
Petra Burka
Canapress Photo Service
Wallace Distelmeyer
Jack Eastwood
Sheldon Galbraith
Holiday on Ice
Ice Capades
Donald Jackson
Maria Jelinek
Barbara Gratton Kelly
Karen Magnussen
Donald McPherson
Cecil Smith
Vern Taylor
Toronto Star

Index